Don't Hide

Jayne Taylor

ISBN 978-0-9574383-0-9

Printed in the U.K. by Charlesworth Press, Flanshaw Way, Flanshaw Lane, Wakefield, WF2 9LP.

Acknowledgements

My *heartfelt thanks and dedication to the truly caring people around me who have been consistently sensitive towards my life, and towards the investment and enormous effort to develop and assemble this book - you've physically, mentally and emotionally put me together too. I have been blessed and privileged to have had each and every one of you cross my path with your help, care, love or gift.*

I'd like to thank my G.P. for their constant involvement and the N.H.S. Thank you also to Pathways - the self-funding outreach programme that provides support, education, safety and counselling services to victims of domestic abuse.

My loving thanks to my sister who, over time, has become my best friend. Thank you to my church, where I continue to grow spiritually in peace and contentment, and its members, who I trust completely. Finally, thank you to Diane, my writing coach; sought out for her guidance, editing and interminable help throughout the writing of this book. She's been an amazing person to work with and has perfectly understood the pain and the heartbreak of my journey, literally feeling every tear and cry.

Foreword

Twenty-four hours from death, and there I lay, on a hospital bed with a burst duodenal ulcer spreading its poison throughout my body.

Voices came and went, and in my state, I wasn't entirely sure where they came from, or if the speakers were in this world or the next. Morphine battled my pain, offering brief respite, but as there was so little flesh on my body, medical staff had to regimentally control the dosage from being fatal.

My four year-old had found me unconscious on the kitchen floor. Undoubtedly scared out of his wits, he'd been clever enough to remember his grandparents' telephone number and hours later, here I was. It was the eve of the new millennium - a time of fresh beginnings, optimism and joy. To me, it was a point where years of violent and emotional abuse had almost resulted in my death.

As midnight drew closer, I became aware of two women passing the end of my bed.

"Look at her...pissed up, taking hospital beds," one said to the other.

Physically, I wasn't able to respond, but mentally, every neuron was screaming at this judgemental pig of a woman. "You've no idea what I've been through," I wanted to yell. My anger had no choice but to course through my veins in partnership with the venom leaking from my ulcer.

Looking back from where I stand today, I can see how misdirected my anger was; how it must seem crazy to anyone else that I could muster up some fight towards two women I'd never met and never would again, than towards the very people who were responsible for my hospital admittance - those I shared my life with and who purported to love me, but who took some sick satisfaction in causing my pain.

* * * * *

It's taken time, determination and my unwavering Christian beliefs to get me to where I am now. I've addressed feelings and memories buried deep inside me; I've now recognised that the cycle of abusive, negative behaviour towards me started from the moment I was born. Subconsciously, I chose the wrong men, but this pattern of behaviour was already inherent and my future, set in stone. Whilst I'm not excusing any of the horrific abuse I've lived through, I have exercised forgiveness, which has taken more strength and faith than I ever thought possible from one human being.

My energy is now spent breaking the cycle of abuse, so that my son doesn't fall into his father's pattern of behaviour, and on educating women and men, young and old, on the horrific effects of domestic violence.

My faith remains very important to me, and because of my beliefs, I know resolutely that I've been put on this earth to deliver this message. I wouldn't change any of the things that have happened to me or any of the pain I've suffered, because then I wouldn't understand how I'm able to help someone else in the same situation.

This book is about my journey, reflection and, hopefully, inspiration. Inside these pages I hope to give you the strength to initially recognise what constitutes a damaging relationship and where you can turn for the tools to both cope with and escape the situation.

Though it may seem unbelievable, if I can help just one person from being minutes from death, at the hands of someone who's meant to love and protect them, then my whole experience will have been worthwhile.

To those readers who, thankfully, have never suffered from the real-time and longer-lasting effects of domestic abuse, I hope my story both educates and motivates you all to support my cause.

Chapter One:
The original bully: My mother, everyone....

With most children, if you encounter a bully in the playground, it's usually your mother who makes everything better.

But what if your mother *was* the bully?

Nowadays, with the media intruding further and further into our homes and lives, it's not uncommon to read of an unwanted pregnancy or neglected, unloved or abused children, far more so than when I was a young girl in the '60s and '70s.

My story, and what you'll read hereon, describes just how damaging mental abuse is. Bruises may fade, but emotional scars shape one's personality, causing worthlessness, inferiority and a compelling need to carry on the cycle of torment because it's easier than smashing it altogether.

It's only now, as I face middle-age, that I can see the relationships I chose, the friends I made and the life I lived until this point, were all shaped from my childhood. Once abuse is accepted at an early age, it becomes ingrained, so when others outside the family unit also inflict abuse and violence, it's an alien concept to victims that they should fight back. Their self-esteem makes them believe that's all they're good for; they believe that's what love is. In my case, I nearly lost my life on various occasions at the hands of those professing to cherish me.

My mother, the first perpetrator, had also been abused as a child but spent her time on this earth consumed by bitterness, frustration and anger stemming from her circumstances. This choice saw the vitriol and violence continue towards another generation; the harder task of learning from past mistakes was consciously ignored, and further lives were damaged as a result.

I've written this story because I want to stop the cycle, not just in my case, but also so that other families trapped in this position recognise the pattern and get the help they need, before their loved ones experience further damage.

For those of you who can indentify with my experiences, I hope this book gives you strength. For those of you who shake your head with disbelief that families can exist like ours, behind closed doors, I hope this book helps you not to judge people - because you don't know what each one of us has lived to see, or what others have inflicted upon them.

They say we all have a story inside us.......well, this is mine.

* * * * * *

How many people exist who can say their own mother took steps during pregnancy to make sure their child never saw the light of day?

It's one thing to say you don't want kids but nearly all mothers who accidentally fall pregnant allow instinct to kick in, and find they protect their child with the same ferocity a mother lion shows for her cub. Even those adamant they're not the maternal type and who take the decision to offer the baby up for adoption of fostering, nurture its existence with nothing more than indifference until the child can be raised by others.

Few try to induce a miscarriage. That's what my mother did to ensure I wasn't born. Her generation couldn't bear the shame of abortion but a miscarriage, instead, was welcome; it brought relief to those who found themselves in a situation they didn't plan and sympathy from those who believed any expectant mother would be devastated at such an occurrence.

My mother drank gin with the sheer intention and

slightly misguided belief that this alone would cause me to die in her womb. Red-hot baths ensued and when neither worked and I continued to cling to life, she tried to stab my birth sac with knitting needles within her. When this failed, she actually threw herself down the stairs. Can you imagine how desperate she must have been to 'get rid'?

Still I clung on, and all she got was a twisted ankle from the fall.

Such determination to purge, and with no remorse or thoughts of the child, I can only now imagine the bitterness she felt when I remained. During pregnancy, she'd told her sister that she felt unnatural, as if there was an alien growing inside her, and later in life, she would remind her whole brood and anyone who listened just how much she never wanted children. In fact, I couldn't begin to count how many times she'd utter, with disdain, the line, "I suffered for you!" She was even proud of how she'd tried to initiate a miscarriage!

At the time she was carrying me, she and my dad owned a greengrocer's shop. They'd lived within the premises, in small rooms at the back of the business. When it was obvious one day that labour had started, my mother paid little notice to the miracle of new life happening inside her. She gave birth to me in the shop, in what was a traumatic delivery, with my father and her own mother present. I nearly suffocated through complications stemming from the labour, further terrifying my nan who had lost a daughter, Jennifer, a generation earlier, in practically identical circumstances.

We now know that the delay in my mother seeking medical attention was a contributing factor to these complications; I can choose to believe this was an accident, but seeing things as I do now, I do wonder if this was another example of Mum's coldness towards her children.

If an example was ever needed, recent research into my mother's past proved her cold and unnatural demeanour - she'd fallen pregnant before having me but naturally (or on purpose) suffered a miscarriage whilst at home on her own. The result was a foetus that came away, which she subsequently wrapped in newspaper until my father returned home. Once he'd learned of the tragedy, Mum discounted his feelings and disposed of what came away by calmly throwing it on the fire.

Minutes after I'd arrived, it was clear that Mum and I both needed hospital treatment but significantly, two ambulances transported us to hospital. Foil warmed me instead of my mother's arms, and we missed those first moments of natural bonding. Whereas other mums parted from their babies, through premature labour or illness, strive to make up for this lost skin-to-skin connection as soon as they're physically able, my mother never bothered.

I was brought home and spent many of my early months in a makeshift baby bouncer that was the potato scales, so that Mum could carry on working in the shop. God-forbid her life should have changed!

When I was two, Mum went on to have twins - again unwanted, and again, the gin, baths and knitting needles were tools to try and fight nature. But nature won, and my twin brother and sister meant Mum's life working in the shop was no longer viable.

The shop was sold and Dad got a job as a HGV driver, meaning he was away a lot of the time and we were at her sole mercy. It meant that her ridicule, her nastiness and violence went unchecked, though my father was almost as afraid of my mother as us children. He gave in to her, seemingly for an easy life, but just as she was overly dominant and uncaring, he was at the opposite end of the scale - meek and dutiful but very loving and kind (when her back was turned).

She was obsessive about cleaning, which wasn't a bad thing, as her mind was far better occupied with thoughts of tasks to complete than the vitriol she could inflict. Every day the windows had to be washed, inside and out, and the whole house had to be vacuumed, which fell mainly to my Dad on top of his job. Never could the window-washing or vacuuming be missed and her cleanliness was almost unhealthy. Jeyes Fluid was always being poured down our drains; our household must have kept the Jeyes' company in business, we used that much of the stuff.

We children couldn't stand on the rug, nor place our feet on the settee, and Dad daren't sit down or pick up a paper without her say-so. He bore the brunt of so much criticism and bitterness from her over the years, I wonder how he stayed. Everything seemed his fault - he got her pregnant, it was his fault we had no money, yet she never stopped to see that we had a decent, clean home - it was undeniably immaculate. Because she never wasted her money, the furniture we had was as pristine years down the line than the day it was bought. The stairs carpet, for instance, never looked anything but brand-new, mainly because we were forcefully discouraged to walk on it any more than we had to, "in case we wore it out".

She washed her hands many times a day; the knock-on effect was that we always felt dirty because our surroundings were so exceptionally clean. Her bad nerves would get her into such a state that only cleaning or manual tasks seemed to calm her.

I remember standing at our back door when I was about six, eating a sweet; absent-mindedly, I'd thrown the discarded wrapper outside.

Mum went absolutely ballistic; she grabbed my neck and bent me towards the fallen paper so hard that my nose was touching the step. "Pick it up," she screamed, which I did, immediately. I remember puzzling, even at that young age, why an act so insignificant should warrant such anger and punishment. It was a sweet wrapper, outside the house - the wind would have moved it on, no one would have died, but Mum's need to have all in order was more powerful than anything I knew.

Our mealtimes were absolutely regimented - sergeants would have envied her control and discipline. Once, I was giggling at something and nothing with my brother and sister when she loomed over us, whipping the table ferociously hard with a metal dog lead. The rest of the meal was in silence.

I wasn't a great meat eater, particularly red meat, but I was forced to eat it. You never argued with Mum, and, knowing no difference, we children accepted her manner and behaviour. We didn't see what we see now: a tiny woman, "four feet eleven, _and a half_" and a megalomaniac intent on power within her unit. She never showed affection - ever. Her idea of showing love was a meal on the table and clean socks in the drawer. If I did anything practical to help her, like lend a hand with caring for my younger siblings, then, "I was a good girl". I constantly sought her approval - her love - and knowing that practical help made her happy, I became dutiful like my father. It was the only time she ever seemed to notice me or appreciate my existence.

To say she was strict was an understatement, but her style of discipline was all we knew. In fact, the first time we ever registered 'violence' was not that which we received from our mother but an incident involving our aunt. My dad's sister had been having an affair and when my mum found out about it she chose not to keep it to herself but told my father. Whatever his reaction was irrelevant, but my aunt didn't take kindly to what she saw as a betrayal of trust and cornered my mother in our house one night. I can remember cowering, frightened out of my skin, as my mother was hit by my aunt. I don't remember if she fought back, given her bombastic personality and fearlessness, I expect so, but my aunt's raging attack somehow seemed much worse than any physical retribution from our mother to us.

Aged five, my mum's urge to control me was evident when she came to monitor me on a daily basis after I started school. I never saw her, or remembered this in any way, but I've been told she watched me through the railings of my playground religiously. Still, at six years of age, she sent me to school with two dummies; a secure soul would see both of these acts as indicative of an over-protective parent, but following how our family lived, I know this as a further sign of dependence and manipulation.

I was a loner at school, perhaps not surprisingly, but I don't recall feeling upset at this - if anything, it was a relief to be in charge of my own thoughts. Physical discipline and reprimands always came when we even stepped out of line a smidgen at home, but Mum's mental coldness seemed far worse.

All I ever wanted was to be loved; sometimes I ached to be hugged, even smiled upon by my mother, but I can never, ever recall her mouth being anything other than downturned. My father did try to show us some affection, which was a very welcome respite, and I've photos of me and him playing with dolls and games. He was very softly spoken and well-liked; everyone took notice of what he had to say because it was so rare he voiced his thoughts and opinions.

A lot of the affection he passed to the twins and I was done with Mum's ignorance. He worked a lot of hours, not that his presence would have stopped Mum's insistence on her cold regime. She always moaned that her nerves were shattered from looking after the three of us on her own, and her moods were unreadable. She could wake up 'that way out' with herself and the tension in the house was very unsettling. We walked on eggshells, so as not to provoke her in any way, and just listened to her going about her business in the house, banging and slamming doors to vent her anger. She could get so worked up and often openly admitted she "could draw blood" on us.

One day, when I was around eight years old, she was getting me ready for a school trip. She was trying to tame my hair into a ponytail because we always had to be turned out as immaculately as the house. I must have bent down to reach for something and she yanked my hair so roughly that I swore without thinking.

I didn't mean to, not in a million years would I have meant Mum to ever hear me swear but the word was already out there. I cowered, terrified, as she brought the brush down on my head so hard it broke in half, still with my ponytail in her hand. All day, on my trip, I was shaking with remorse and fear, running over and over in my mind that she'd not talk to me, and how horrible a child I must be to have done such a thing as swear at her. This was the level of manipulation - at eight, she could have hospitalised me yet I worried what I'd done to her! I dreaded going home that day, dreaded her wrath, and whether further retribution awaited my return.

The teachers on the trip that day had to come looking for me when it was time to return, finding me in a cathedral. I'd bought a book on St. Luke and St. John and on opening it, I immediately saw the words, "Jesus helps broken people." Reading this somehow made it a little easier to go back home and face her.

It's a given that her patience was short, but her rejection could last days. If you dared to offend her or resist her control she would freeze you out for days and the silent treatment made you feel like an outsider in your own home. I always strived to please her when I was out of favour, desperate to regain peace, so I'd help even more around the house or with the twins which seemed to work. Before long would come the critical words and insults: "I'll put you in care!". Shockingly, this seemed actually a step up from no words at all!

I remember bringing home a slip from school one day saying I'd received detention. She hit me, which wasn't unusual, but what I hated more was the fact I'd disappointed her; I was mortified.

I think I took the brunt of Mum's criticism and bitterness, as my sister and brother didn't seem to abide by her rules as much nor crave her attention so fervently. My brother, especially, didn't receive treatment as harsh as mine as my mother was very much a 'man's woman'.

My sister, Julie, however, was very rebellious - in fact, she flouted her untidiness, seemingly without a care to the consequences. She'd get expelled from school for fighting and even pretended she couldn't see her schoolwork due to her bad eyesight, though nothing was wrong with her vision. She didn't seem to be fazed about lying or causing trouble, but what role model did we have?

There was one time with my sister that sticks out in my mind. She'd argued back to Mum about something then stormed off upstairs, banging the door. She'd slammed this glass door with such force that it had shattered. As penance, Mum made my sister sell all her 'Tiny Tears' collection of dolls and the paraphernalia she'd amassed form birthdays and Christmas presents, to pay for replacing the glass.

There was no way Mum threatened anything then backed down, so my sister had to go through with getting rid of her whole collection, but I remember she didn't cry. She wouldn't show Mum how upset she was.

Whilst it's clear I took after my father, my sister was so like my mum. Even now, my sister has anxiety problems akin to OCD, and when they lived in the same house, they'd rub each other up the wrong way because they were so alike. My brother-in-law has said he could "dance on Mum's grave" for the problems and issues my sister's left with. She has never forgiven Mum for what we went through as children - she didn't keep up a relationship with her in adulthood - though they did make some sort of peace just before Mum died.

I didn't defy Mum often, as you can imagine, but

I can remember an incident when I was twelve. Mum had warned me who I could play with; her threat of, "If I ever see you with any lads, I'll break your back!" always resounded in my head, but it seemed plain to me at that age that girls and boys could be in each other's company quite innocently. I waited until Dad and the twins had gone for a drive with the dog to some public walkway before joining a group of people I knew from school. It was quite freeing to be doing something exciting, and I soon forgot about the fact I wasn't even supposed to be there. Only when I saw Dad's car turn the corner did I panic and run home to be punished - humiliated and embarrassed at Dad's shouting through the wound-down window of the trouble I was in.

Although I believed Mum's behaviour was no different than that of other families when I was very young, I saw flashes of normal parental behaviour during primary school. Other kids' parents seemed so permanently chilled out; I saw other parents kissing their kids and ached for the same kind of affection from my mother. I can't tell you how much I wanted to hear the words, "I love you", but I knew I'd be waiting forever - it took her all her time to even be nice to me. Even at this young age, I remember thinking that if I ever had children I'd shower them with affection - I vowed never to treat them in the same way my mother treated me.

It annoyed me how she always saw the worst in people, she was never prepared to give anyone a chance. As I was so eager to please and craved affection from anyone, I just saw the best of people, but perhaps went too far and appeared needy. Mum tried to bestow her narrow-minded views: "People take advantage," she'd say. Perhaps writing them off immediately, in her mind, saved her from any disappointment later.

I never brought any of my girl friends back home as a child as I couldn't explain the scrutiny and insults they'd hear or receive. My mother judged everyone, she never had a kind word to say, there was always something the matter with all others but not her.

She'd antagonise people too. She had names for all the neighbours, calling one "Little Runt" to his face many times. She took it upon herself to move his washing for some reason one day, and when he challenged her, she just told him to "Fuck off!". People around us were scared of her, and she never held back from hurling insults, saying to one neighbour that, "her gob was as big as her fanny". On a short trip to London, I remember her physically hurling her coffee at the waitress because it had been served colder than she liked.

Even in her later years, when she suffered complications from her years of smoking and endured the restrictions her narrowing airways gave, she still had the same fight. One relapse saw the family call an ambulance to the house, and when asked by the paramedic whether she could walk to the vehicle, she answered, "Does it look like I can fucking walk?".

After being warned her smoking habit was seriously harming her health, she wouldn't take medical advice - she'd rather have died then and there than take heed of anyone's opinions other than her own.

This bloody-mindedness was sometimes put to good use. Though half his size, she stopped and detained a twenty-four year old thief with her walking stick in Jonathan James' shoe shop until the police arrived. He probably was struck down more with shock than physical fear, given that she wasn't even five feet tall!

Although physically and mentally abusive to my siblings and I, this was mostly behind closed doors; she didn't make a point of showing it off in the streets. Out shopping in Barnsley, she spotted a father swiping his toddler's head with the back of his knuckle; she crossed the road to get to him and threatened the father with the police if she saw him do it again. One push from this hulking man would have seen her flat out on the floor but she wasn't afraid of anything or anyone. He seemed ready to fly at her for poking her nose in, but backed down once he'd got a measure of her viciousness.

There were times when she seemed to want to play happy families, like when we were on holiday. You'd never have called her a saint but she seemed to relax more, and with Dad there to shoulder the 'burden' as she'd refer to us, she wasn't quite as moody. We'd go on days out as a family or stay in caravans, which were still kept meticulously, obsessively clean and tidy, despite being miles from home and her regime.

I truly loved those holidays as we seemed more like other people. Coming back home and it was back to reality, back to Mum's snide and bitter remarks, with everyone bending over backwards to keep her happy.

It's hard to understand how she could be such a Jekyll and Hyde character. When we were away I could believe she'd changed, but practically before we'd got through the door she'd start again. Then came one of the most shocking things I remember about her that proved we weren't normal, and that she didn't think like other people.

As we got a little older and found interests outside the home through friends and school it became clear to her that she was losing a little of her control. I remember her having to go into hospital then recall being gathered around her bed with the rest of the family. There, she broke the news she had breast cancer.

Despite everything, we were devastated. My brother wanted answers and information as to how to look after her and what - if anything - could be done. He left her bedside and collared a nurse.

After asking her when we'd know more about Mum's treatment - or even if her cancer could indeed be treated - there was a look of confusion on the nurse's face.

"Cancer? Your mum hasn't got cancer. She had a couple of harmless lumps in her breast but we've taken them out."

Unbelievably, this was never mentioned again. Not one of us, despite my brother telling us the truth away from Mum's glare, ever brought the subject up or asked her why she'd lied - right up until the day she died. We didn't dare.

Mum developed rheumatoid arthritis from the age of thirty-five and claimed she'd been given a raw deal in life, constantly bemoaning, "Why me?". She always spoke disparagingly of her sisters, who she claimed she'd practically raised. She saw that they had nice houses, new cars, and believed they had a better life than her self-inflicted drudgery. What she couldn't see was that she had a lovely family, a loving husband and a house so pristine it could shine in the dark. Although we didn't have much money coming into our household, Mum was great at making it stretch as far as it would go. She took pride in making the best of what she had, in practical terms. The furniture and her belongings were well-chosen and looked after, staying at their best; her relationships with her sisters, well, they weren't close. Living far apart, the sisters would make arrangements to get together in one place but never rung my mother. Whether she even knew about this, or if this hurt her, she never said.

Neither did Mum have friends outside the home, (she never seemed to count those inside it as friends either). She was always so angry about her hard life, of how she ended up with three children when she didn't want any at all. It's obvious that my temperament mirrors my father's - keeper of the peace, pliant, a kind soul who just wanted to serve and please others. Although Mum's manipulative control, cruel words and violence kept me introverted, repressed and shy, I found my salvation at the age of nine.

My first school was run by the church, and I joined the choir around this time, finding it so uplifting that I started to attend church every Sunday. It does seem strange to me, even now, that my mother could force me to eat things I didn't want, to do things I didn't want and treated me so brutally that I was often fearful to be in her company, yet when I went to church each week I found the strength to override her derision. She ridiculed my interest in the church yet I was unwavering, continuing to go each Sunday and learn more about Jesus and his faith. I'd get myself up and dressed, still only really a young child, to sing in the church choir each week. I loved singing there - it felt good to finally have a voice and be encouraged to express it. I loved the sermons too, they seemed so familiar to me. They seemed to spell out exactly what I was thinking.

I wanted, more than anything, a world filled with love - I couldn't understand why people like Mum were so negative and horrible. I was willing to trust and be a friend to all I met and couldn't fathom why I seemed to be in the minority.

It certainly wasn't a duty to attend church, like some of the people who went; I was so passionate about church that I couldn't wait to go again each time I came out. Although people and families showed up each Sunday they seemed blasé about being there which made me quite mad sometimes. Why couldn't they see what I saw? Why didn't other people care for others like I did?

I took my cousin, Theresa, when I was twelve and she was four - I was independent and mature even then. She seemed to quite enjoy it and I was happy I could share church - I would have taken everyone in the whole world had they been interested. Theresa only came with me for a short while, though, before her family moved away.

The feeling of belonging to something so pure and giving is quite indescribable. When those in my life, up to that point, had never told me how much I was loved and accepted, when all I had was their anger and criticism, there was little wonder I responded so positively to the Christian faith. I felt free, safe; I felt I belonged in church, that this was my real 'home'. I could identify with the readings, and felt that some were actually talking directly to me. For instance, Jesus' walk with the cross towards his crucifixion, when he had so much disgust and fierce rage thrown at him from the jeering crowds lining the street, yet still he continued to forgive - although more than two thousand years separated us, it could have been me they were talking about. I knew exactly how he'd have felt.

"Jesus was gathered and clothes stripped off him, a scarlet robe put on him then a crown made of thorns, it was placed on his head, he was mocked, spat at, hit with a stick and the crown of thorns drew blood. They cast insults then they crucified him" **Matthew 27:31**

People in church were warm, they didn't judge, they only wanted to support me. I wasn't responsible for keeping everyone happy like I was forced to at home, as people at church were genuinely kind, compassionate and accepting. They didn't ridicule me or keep me down; instead, they gave me strength and helped me find solace and strength.

After some time, I wanted to take bread and wine at the altar with the others at church. I wanted to show my commitment and understanding of the symbolism to what this act meant. However, it had never crossed my mind that I wasn't christened which meant I couldn't do this; after nearly six years of pleading my mother, I was confirmed by the Archbishop of Sheffield in my teens. My mother didn't waste the chance to ridicule me. "When are you becoming a nun?" she'd spit. It really grated on her that the one thing I was prepared to stand up and fight for was my faith. She found it hard to be critical of something so positive (though she tried damned hard) which annoyed her further. She said that on school trips, you'd only be able to find me if you searched the nearest church or cathedral but it was plain she was jealous of the draw the church held for me.

I can remember playing games of 'Holy Communion' with my brother, acting out the process of taking the bread and wine; I was completely innocent of the fact not all people saw the church as something wonderful. Mum's treatment of me had, from a young age, caused me to withdraw from adults, yet at church I didn't display these reservations. At home, I always strived to be 'the good girl', yet it went either unnoticed or unrewarded. Church promoted inner goodness and charity, so it was no surprise I felt more at home there than anywhere else.

I had this unwavering feeling that God was looking out for me, despite all I suffered at the hands and mind of my mum. I could sometimes hear a voice inside, especially when I needed help or guidance - and still do, to this day. Signs and signals accompanied me, reassured me and made me feel as if I wasn't alone. The twins had each other, even my mum had my dad, so I suppose I could have been excused for feeling isolated - but that's the thing - I never did feel alone once I'd found God.

My creativity blossomed as I started to find a confidence away from my mother. Unsurprisingly, I excelled at religious studies at school but I also channelled a lot of my feelings into anything creative - such as artwork, crafts or writing. I became quite the perfectionist, which may have been inherent from my mother's obsessive and compulsive tendencies, but used this attention to detail positively, to better my education. Looking back, I think I was driven by a need to be appreciated.

My faith was stronger than the hold my mother had over me. Although she ridiculed my commitment, I didn't let her words affect me. My faith gave me a shield that she couldn't penetrate. She could abuse and insult anything else in my life, but if she ever derided my faith or my church, her words just washed over me like water from a duck's back.

If children live with criticism, they learn to condemn
If children live with hostility, they learn to fight
If children live with shame, they learn to feel guilty
If children live with tolerance, they learn to be patient
If children live with encouragement, they learn confidence
If children live with praise, they learn to appreciate
If children live with fairness, they learn justice
If children live with security, they learn to have faith
If children live with approval, they learn to like themselves
If children live with acceptance and friendship, they learn
to find love in the world

Dorothy Nolte

This epitomises the church versus my mother. Mum was all criticism and hostility whereas church was encouraging, approving, accepting and welcoming - there was no contest. Jesus loved me and this just added to her bitterness.

By my late teens her views were getting more offensive; for example, she thought that it was Kylie Minogue's own fault that she got breast cancer because, "she must have been fondling herself too much".

She thought depressed people should "pull themselves together", and never showed any compassion for anyone. Mum's beliefs were almost Victorian, and her generation wasn't completely to blame for this. She never showed any flesh or even exposed her arms, and sex seemed disgusting to her. I can imagine she was a, "turn the lights off, think of England and it will all be over quickly," type, and Dad wasn't allowed to even physically touch her when she was pregnant. She didn't seem to ever have any fun, the only thing she ever found anywhere near relaxing was a spot of gardening. Whilst her sisters seemed to enjoy a good life, not just in the material sense, you got the impression that my mother only tolerated or endured her existence.

She got worse with age (should you be able to

imagine this). My brother and sister found their partners at a very young age and didn't need any persuading to leave home. I made friends in my teens and started to go to pubs and nightclubs. Although I enjoyed going out, I didn't like getting drunk; I didn't like the feeling of losing control and stood my ground as my friends tried to cajole me into chucking the stuff down my neck.

I always felt more mature than my friends, and could never let go and act the silly sod. Life wasn't light-hearted enough for me to be daft; I always took things more seriously than I should have done at that age. My friends were snogging boys each weekend and dancing until dawn whereas I was still governed by my manipulative mother in early adulthood and thought church, not the bottom of a beer bottle, was my sanctuary. I can understand why this seemed a little strange to my peers.

I had some good friends by this time, Michelle and Donna. I'd take them back home, which was a sign I was getting more defiant with age, and was quite surprised to find my friends liked my mum. If I'm truthful, both Michelle and Donna were very opinionated and had strong personalities. I think Mum backed down and didn't ridicule them because they weren't afraid of her - in fact, they had many facets of their personalities in common. All of them took charge over me and didn't give me a voice.

Church was still the mainstay in my life, and the only place I could truly be myself and not have anyone try and manipulate me or put me down. When I was twenty-two, Dr. Billy Graham, an evangelist from America, was coming to my hometown for the week and the organisers were putting on free buses for people to go and hear him talk. On my own, I went every day of that week and felt moved on one night in particular.

There'd been an array of guest speakers appearing alongside Dr. Graham but on this one night Sir Cliff Richard gave a talk on his Christian life. His testimony resonated with me and I came away a different person than when I'd arrived - I literally felt as if I'd been reborn. I physically felt God there that night, right inside my heart. For the first time in my life I knew the type of person I wanted to be wasn't who my mother thought I was. She thought I was good for nothing, someone to push around. She never got to enjoy the loving, kind person I actually was because she always pushed me away or treated me badly.

It may sound strange that up until then, even though I was in my early twenties, I was still so controlled by my mum, or that I still yearned for her appreciation and love. You'd imagine that I'd have wised up after all those years but I'd always made excuses for her; I constantly believed she would change one day. That night, I realised she never would.

"A prayer of confidence: Protect me O God, I trust in you for my safety. I say to the Lord, 'You are my Lord', all the good things I come from you" **Psalms 16**

Chapter Two:
The lengths I'd go to, just to please...

Despite this realisation, what happened next in my life was still further proof of my mother's gripping hold.... the fact I married my first husband just to please her.

In my late teens I'd planned to go to Australia and stay with my uncle (my mum's brother) and aunt. I'd got into the hairdressing trade by then and planned to work with my cousin for six months over there. I'd got it all sorted, secured the visa and saved my money, even paid board.

Mum went crazy. She bitterly criticised the opportunity from day one, which wasn't surprising, and dampened my enthusiasm by making me fearful of anything foreign. Her scaremongering escalated as I continued to plan for the trip, borne from her own fear that I would be out of her control. She didn't want to lose her emotional punch-bag.

Around the same time, my aunt tried to set me up with someone she knew, Richard, who had his own hairdressing salon. Once my aunt mentioned him, that was it, my mother relentlessly urged me to go out with him. She even enrolled my brother to help push the guy onto me.

"He's a nice lad, got his own business - he'll take care of you," she'd say. "Give him a chance."

The fact of the matter was that this guy, Richard, made my skin crawl. He wasn't nasty but there wasn't an inch of him that appealed. There was no spark, no attraction for me, but my aunt and brother, and especially my mum, nagged me so much that I gave in to a date with him just for a quiet life.

Richard was even creepier than I'd taken him for. He was very touchy-feely and set my teeth on edge. I knew as soon as the first date had started that I didn't want a second.

Even then, I think I suspected that my mother's keenness to pair me off was just another ploy to stop me from fleeing to Australia. I'd be here, still available for emotional manipulation, not a thousand miles away building a new life. Richard was also someone she could push around; he was meek and mild, and respected what she said, even if it was to his detriment or outwardly critical.

I came back from the first date and said, "There's no way I want to see him again," but days of, "he'll grow on you," wore me down. In Mum's eyes, it didn't matter that he made me shiver with disgust, you didn't need to like someone to be with them. She painted him as this heaven-sent creature that would look after me and care for me - who would give me the love and devotion she knew I'd craved since birth.

I'd spent a lifetime trying to please Mum and keep her happy. I'd spent most of my waking days walking on eggshells so as not to upset her, and trying my damndest to show her she could love me. I'd always been a good girl, always tried to care for her, despite years of rejection and cruelty, yet I still went back for more. Against my wishes and desires, I carried on dating Richard. I can remember thinking that my relationship would surely please her.

Whenever he kissed me I was truly repulsed. It felt so wrong and horrible. As for sex, it only happened when I felt sorry for him. Because sometimes, I did, though I never instigated anything physical. At times I realised the irony; that his devotion to me even when I treated him horribly was similar to the relationship I had with my mother. Although I couldn't help myself, I did recognise that he wasn't a horrible person, and that I had the issues. But one thing I clearly did resent was when he accompanied me to church. Church was my sanctuary, away from all that was unpleasant in my life. It had been my refuge and respite when Mum had decided to play with my mind and it was also good to escape the confines of my unhappy marriage, but when Richard came I felt territorial. He probably only had good intentions and just wanted to share something that was obviously very important to me, but I felt his accompaniment infringed on my privacy.

After so long, and so much badgering from my family, I even started telling myself that Richard would grow on me, and, with the Australia plan seemingly 'parked', I carried on dating him as I knew it was what my mother wanted.

To be perfectly honest, I don't remember really making a conscious decision about it all. I just took one day at a time and felt numb about the situation. My sister and brother had both settled down and left home so it just seemed a natural progression that Mum wanted to pair me off too.

Six months down the line I was still dating Richard when he proposed. This did make me take notice, because I knew that there was no way I was ever going to love him or have any strong feelings for him, on any spectrum. I told Richard that I'd think about it (not that I needed to) - it was the kindest way of stalling him. I couldn't bring myself to say what I really felt.

As soon as I told Mum she spent nearly every waking hour trying to talk me into marrying him. I was in my twenties, "she could finally get shut". She just wore me down and before long, I was in the registry office saying, "I do".

There were no big, dramatic moments on the day of the wedding, no last-minute realisation or me screaming, "What am I doing?". I was very calm; I didn't attach any importance to the day at all. Though we were stood in front of the registrar, we could just have easily been stood queuing for cinema tickets or shopping in the supermarket for all the energy and emotion I exerted. It was telling that we didn't get married in church - I think that would have made it all real; I know I would have felt differently blatantly lying about my feelings in front of God, as my faith only continued to be precious to me. Neither was any member of our families invited, because the day didn't register as something to celebrate nor resemble an occasion. I didn't feel attached to Richard, he could have been a work colleague, a friend of a friend or the postman, such was my distance.

I used any excuse to get away from him once we were married. I had friends in Nottingham who I'd visit most weekends - far enough away that it meant staying over. Mum would find out and scream, "What kind of wife are you?"; my weekends away sparked terrible anger within her. If I ever tried to tell her how trapped and unhappy I felt in my marriage she'd go crazy. Dad would feel sorry for me and understood my predicament but she wholly blamed me for the fact my marriage was a failure and never recognised she may have pushed me into it.

I stayed married to Richard for seven years, and finally found the strength through my faith to do what I should have done at the beginning, which was to stand up for myself. I had seen in church what love could be and knew I was never going to experience this whilst I stayed with him. Maturity also played its part and I knew if I stayed, accepting the situation, I'd end up treating Richard really badly which wouldn't have been fair on him at all. I knew that ending our marriage would be better for both of us in the long run.

"Finally build up your strength in union with the Lord and by means of his mighty power, put on all the armour that God gives you so that you will be able to stand against the wicked rules" **Ephesians 6, verse 10**

When I told Richard he left the house straightaway, but we also had two businesses together. I wasn't bothered about fighting for things in the divorce; once I'd made the decision to please myself and not others I just wanted to move on and walk away. I actually had to fight with my solicitor not to take Richard to the cleaners! I eventually kept the house and the mortgage but all I felt was relief that I was free from the marriage.

Telling my mother about all this had been harder than telling Richard - it just gave her more ammunition to insult me, deride me and make me feel worthless. She told me to "get back there, lie down and think of England!". She fell out with me - which was another of her mind games. She was punishing me for having a mind of my own and 'froze me out' for over a year. During this time, Richard still visited Mum. I conceded that this was more to do with the strong hold she'd also had over him but I imagined they'd have been sat like witches, cackling, "Poor Richard, fancy having to put up with a wife like her."

Eventually, I went to her. I knew hell would have frozen over before she'd have come to me. Even though she'd not spoken to me throughout those months, I'd not felt as liberated as you may imagine. Instead, I felt guilty - guilty that we were fighting, guilty that I'd 'caused' so much upset. She was on my mind constantly and I spent the whole year feeling as if I was in the wrong, even though I clearly felt I'd been pushed into the relationship and subsequent marriage. I lived day to day and didn't look at the bigger picture. Because I still didn't recognise her cruelty and the bitterness she projected as being her fault, it meant that even though we were apart, I didn't properly heal or gain enough strength to actually challenge her. I didn't get rid of the fear.

Although she wouldn't see things from my point of view when I went to see her, and even though I still felt fear, I think she could tell I was slightly stronger now. I still tried to please her, but knew I didn't have to stay to listen to her criticism. When the petrol strike was on ten years ago, I desperately wanted to go to church and was offered a lift but my mum didn't want me to go. I went anyway and she was absolutely livid that she's not been able to control the situation or get her own way as she'd been used to.

I really enjoyed living on my own. Being a loner throughout my life meant I was fine with my own company. I didn't crave companionship - in fact, I was glad to be left alone! It took time to rebuild the relationship with Mum - even though I'd made that first move and gone to seek her forgiveness, she didn't let me off lightly, and it was months before we were 'normal' again. She'd still deride me, saying, "I've had three kids but it's only you who's brought trouble to my door."

Mum still had to keep tabs on me though. Even in my late twenties, she'd call me, telling me what time I'd turned my lights off in the flat. It was back to the school railings again, the monitoring, the twisted interest in what I was doing away from her clutches. She'd phone many times a day, and I'd have to explain what I'd had for tea. This could be construed as a mother only wanting to ensure her child was taking care of herself but I knew it wasn't like that - it felt as if I was clocking in and clocking out.
If she came round to the flat, it was like being on trial. Her obsessive cleaning always made me feel my domestic abilities were never as good as hers and she'd constantly vet and judge everything, even the contents of my fridge. She drained the life out of me; on my own, I could see a future, be positive, I could almost feel free. But when I was with her, I was back to being five years old again, scrutinised and fearful. She could trigger the same feelings of worthlessness within me, even though I was nearly thirty years of age.

The violence, of course, stopped as I got older and physically capable of resisting or retaliating. But the emotional abuse was actually far worse. It was constant - lasting longer than any hard slap and hurt far more. I don't think I felt free of her mental cruelty until the day she died.

Strangely, according to my aunt, I was her favourite.

This, I've always struggled to believe. The twins always seemed to escape her abuse, so I always considered them to be loved far more than I was. They also seemed stronger because they had each other and were more of a match than me, being tiny and delicate at best. She certainly seemed more obsessed about me, as she didn't monitor or try to control my siblings as intensively. In fact, the level of rebellion my sister showed made me uncomfortable - I felt sure she'd be severely punished and abused each time but she seemed to get away with her defiance.

I only ever tried to be the good one. I took after my father in always trying to please others and only seeing the best in them.

You'd have thought then, that I'd be dumbfounded at Mum's behaviour but it didn't once shock me. It knew it was unpleasant, uncalled for and unchallenged but she'd never, ever shown another side to her character.
So it came as quite a shock, many years later, and a few years after her death, when I was stopped by an elderly lady who I didn't recognise, in the salon I ran at the time.

"How's your dad?" the old lady asked. My father, at this point, had also died not so long ago, about a year after Mum.

"We lost him," I said.

"How about your mum?" she continued.

I told the lady we'd lost her too, at which point, she started to sob.

"Your mum was lovely," she said.

Apparently, Mum had met the lady when they'd both been waiting for a hospital appointment. She'd made such an impact on this woman, who went on to say she'd spoken only of me when they'd talked. The woman had been that taken by Mum's enthusiasm and the warm way she'd described me that she'd never forgotten her, and which that day, saw her specifically trace my salon to meet me in person.

Whilst Dad's funeral had been packed out, Mum's had been sparse with guests. Although she'd not had friends and even the relationships with her family had been fraught, we gave her, I think, a warm send off.

Mum and I had actually got the closest we'd ever been in the months before her death, as is often the case. She'd been so ill with her lung problems and had struggled for each that she'd needed others to care for her. She'd let me near her then, when she was vulnerable, and it was almost as if our roles had changed; she'd become the child and I, the parent. At this late stage in her life we'd actually said, "I love you" to each other, though we never talked about why she'd treated me so badly. It upset her to admit her motherly love - I think it brought home to her how weak and exposed she was, whereas I, even after all she'd done, thought it was lovely to get so close to her.

It's only now, years after her death, and after everything I've lived through since, that I can begin to forgive her bitterness, but as a mother myself now, I do find it hard to understand. She'd had a horrible childhood too, at the hands of my grand-dad, but she was also responsible for her own actions. She had a choice, just as I have, not to let what has been done to me affect how I treat others.

If she had made the right choice when carrying me - if she'd made the decision to protect, nurture and love me at all costs - perhaps I may have made different choices too, with the men in my life. It could all have been so different, her constant insults could have been affirmations of love. I could have celebrated being loved and my self-esteem would have been far healthier.

My need to be loved wouldn't have been there, or as intensely acute. But it was, and this simple fact was taken advantage of, to the point I almost died.

Chapter Three:
Does anyone love me?

Now that Richard was no longer a part of my life, I felt less constrained. Mum still had a huge hold over me, even as I approached my thirties, but freedom was nearer to my grasp than it had ever been.

I had thought that getting divorced from Richard would solve all my problems, and that I could 'heal' from the emotional and mental abuse showered on me from my mother. My self-esteem was so battered, I didn't know what feeling 'normal' was; whenever I went out I was jealous of everyone. Not because they were part of a couple or anything, but because anyone I came across seemed so 'together' while I just felt a wreck. I felt as though there was something wrong with me.

As a diversion, I threw myself into my hairdressing business and building up the salon's reputation. It was all I had in life and it did really well. I always made sure it was more than just a haircutting service whenever anyone walked through the door. I just felt that each person could have had a crappy day or seemingly insurmountable issues and that their appointment in my salon may have been the first time that week they were able to gather their thoughts or offload their stress, so it became almost a counselling service with a haircut thrown in. I had people hunting the salon down through word of mouth, and I made sure all my staff gave the same committed service. My desire to 'give, give, give' had not been diminished, despite Mum and Richard.

After a few months I started socialising again with my girlfriends; we'd go for a drink and a gossip. Men were the furthest thing from my mind after the mess with Richard but six months or so after the divorce, I met David in a wine bar.

I definitely did not go out looking for anyone; I'd felt freer than ever before and, if you discounted my mother's control, I was finally able to please myself in life. But David charmed me, showered me with affection and compliments. He was quite full on, but everything he said was what I'd always longed to hear. I was hugely flattered. "A guy wants me?!" I thought. I didn't agree to go out with him at first but I did give him my number. Immediately, he was phoning what felt like a hundred times a day, desperate to make me go out with him.

I really didn't see this, at the time, as a form of control - I just thought David really, really liked me. He was different to Richard, and very attractive - tall, dark, tanned. He took care of himself and he didn't make my skin crawl!

"But what could he want with me? I'm five years older than him, for starters," I wondered. I won't deny that his attention was a boost to my ego. Whether this slight age gap was responsible for the desire to nurture I experienced or whether it was just my genetic mapping - I just wanted to care for someone....and have someone care about me.

I gave in to my optimism and we started courting. David was twenty-five and still living at home with his parents. Although he showered me with gifts, wining and dining me at the very beginning of our relationship, it wasn't long - about three weeks, in fact - before I was the one paying for drinks and for dinner. Neither was it long before the relationship's dynamics shifted to me giving and David 'taking, taking, taking'.

After just a short time, I saw a very different side to him. One particular day, early in our relationship, we were at a friend's house and he appeared moody. Despite me persistently asking, "What's wrong?" his temper didn't improve. A familiar feeling washed over me and I instantly felt uneasy. I spent the day walking on eggshells, like I did around my mother when she was in one of her moods. At the same time, a voice rang loudly in my head, saying, "Get out while you can! Go, now!"

The words I heard I recognised as my intuition, which often made its appearance in times of stress or trouble. David was continuing to bang about, just like Mum when she slammed doors, so my automatic, ingrained thought was, "What have I done?". You'll notice, no blame was on David; surely the whole shift in his mood must have been my fault.

His 'Prince Charming' demeanour had vanished and I didn't dare ask him why. I felt fearful, intimidated.

This, I concede, would be enough for the majority of men or women to call time on the relationship, however fledgling it may be. But my mental conditioning overpowered my common sense and I inwardly vowed to change him, to help him return to the nice person I'd seen he could be. I gave myself another chance to gain his acceptance, just as I had many, many times with Mum throughout my childhood, and therefore chose not to walk away at the sound of my own warning bells but instead, choosing to persevere.

As you'll read on, you'll undoubtedly question why I stayed when so many signs were pointing, right from the outset, how much danger I'd placed myself in, or that David was unlikely to change - my mother's personality should have shown me that. I look back now and, of course, it's blindingly obvious, but at the time I genuinely thought that I'd healed from all the abuse and mind games my mother had exposed me to and that I was stronger - capable of turning someone like David into someone like me.

He'd told me that he'd been the victim of an abusive relationship as he'd grown up; his dad had been violent many times to his mother. He'd been exposed to terrible bouts of anger and aggression and assumed he'd been brought up a victim. Neither of us realised, at this early point, just how well he'd learned to be an abuser.

Despite these moods, six months on, we were living together. He'd moved into my nice house, bought from the ongoing success of the salon, and life seemed to be on a relatively even keel. David liked nice things and grooming himself, buying clothes and boys' toys, with my money. He always "had to have this" and demanded the best, from motorbikes to cars and all the accessories that went with them. In his mind, his wage was his; I was there to provide and if he didn't get his own way, the sulks would appear. And I just wanted to please him.

We went out one night, not long after he'd moved in with me, for a nice meal and a drink when he decided that another guy was definitely looking at me. He started getting annoyed, saying, "What's he fucking looking at?" I tried my best to calm David down but a fight broke out between them. One of David's hobbies was kick-boxing which meant he left the guy accused of eyeing me up unconscious.

"Get in the fucking car!" he snarled.

I was desperate not to inflame things further so I got in the car I'd bought him and we roared off.

David's nickname amongst his friends was 'Taz', short for 'Tasmanian Devil', as he was well-known for his temper. He was driving at such a terrifying speed and I begged him to slow down - at one point, the car was balancing on two wheels as we screeched through streets at 50-60mph. I was so frightened and kept begging him to stop but as he drove, he grabbed me by my hair and banged my head against the inside of the car door.

Before I could gather my thoughts, and whilst still driving at breakneck speed, he opened the car door and pushed me out. We must have been doing 70mph.

I was left bloody, bruised and cut on the grass verge as he sped off. It took time to catch my breath but I felt sure nothing was broken, though even if it had been, I was too scared to go to hospital. I was dazed and terrified, I didn't even dare move. If felt as if I was there for hours but it was probably only 10-20 minutes before David returned, absolutely remorseful.

He was sorry, he said, he didn't know what came over him. He just wanted to protect me because he loved me so much. He would change to make sure it never happened again. He kept repeating that he didn't know what had got into him, that it was through his fear of losing me that had made him act that way. Never once did he consider how scared I'd been, or still was, sat on that verge. No, the moment was all about him.

* * * * * * *

It is easy, as an outsider to someone else's relationship, to definitely say what's right or wrong, or whether it's the best decision for two people to stay together. Although I recognised David's behaviour and the balance of our relationship was wrong, my belief that he could overcome all his issues far outweighed my negative thoughts. I *wanted* to believe he wouldn't do anything like that again, and having spent the whole of my life believing my mother would change, appreciate me or show me love, this felt no different.

I sat on that grass verge so weak that I couldn't fight my nurturing instinct; I wasn't strong enough to face telling David to leave or to stand up for myself. I got back in the car and we drove to David's mother's house.

I don't remember if she asked what had happened or if it was blatantly obvious that something was badly wrong, but once the story came out (from David's viewpoint, of course), she said to me, "Well Jayne, you know what his temper's like," as if it was my fault.

She went on to tell me that David had been violent to her in the past; he'd got angry about something and smashed the kitchen up, holding his mum against the wall with a table leg to her throat. At that moment, I felt she'd excused his behaviour, just like all those times David's father had gone ballistic too.

David went up to bed with no shame. *It was done, over with, time to move on.*

After a few days all was back to an even keel, the incident unmentioned. I never once thought David couldn't be saved from himself, and firmly believed, now the fear had subsided, that I was the one to show him the way.

I managed to hide my physical scratches and bruises gained when pushed from the car from my family and especially from my mum. She couldn't stand David, thought he was a bit of a poser and show-off, and she would have gloated until the cows came home at what he'd done to me.

I knew from my faith that what David had done was a sin but if he could ignore it and pretend it never happened then it seemed so should I. Although part of me was optimistic that because he regretted it so much he'd make sure there were no repeat incidents, it was exhausting living with him. I didn't know what mood he'd come home in and I had to make sure I never said anything or did anything that would set his temper off again. Added to that, I was working all hours in the business to pay for his clothes, cars, bikes, as well as all the bills. I had to sell my lovely sports car, which I'd been so proud of owning, to fund his spending.

David went out a lot with his friends, whenever he wanted, and when he did, I had to stay in so he knew where I was. I felt terribly lonely. He was controlling and I tried to justify his actions with the thought that he was protecting me from any danger. I just accepted his instructions; whatever he demanded he always got, and the more I gave him, the more he wanted.

The house didn't have a garage and when he came

home with a new motorbike one day that didn't fit in our shed, he smashed up the wooden hut in a rage, such was his reaction if things didn't go his way.

By this time, his temper was getting worse. Two to three times a week he was either slapping me or knocking me around. Each time he was sorry, he'd never do it again, but the 'up/down, up/down' nature of his moods was literally crippling me.

The physical abuse was repeated over and over again; another incident occurred when he'd wrongly assumed a guy was looking at me. David shoved me into the car for another ride of terror. This time, though, I jumped out at some traffic lights, as I knew he wouldn't hesitate to push me out again and I might not be as lucky to walk away with just cuts and bruises again.

I thought I'd escaped the confrontation but he turned the car round and came back for me, chasing me down. He pinned me up against a lamp-post by my throat - my feet were actually lifted from the ground. I was choking and saw a red mist literally appear on his face. He didn't care whether we were in full view or if we could be seen, he'd lost it.

I was struggling to breathe and kicked with all my might. I was tiny, so it didn't take much exertion for a big, strong guy like him to lift me up in the air. Eventually he let me go, but he could so easily have kept on squeezing.

I tried to leave him after that, a few times. He'd go back to his mother's and I'd stay in the house, heartbroken. I knew what love was meant to be like, I'd studied and felt it so much in church, that I truly believed I could make David see that a loving relationship didn't have to involve such violence or abuse.

I even attended counselling, on my own. I'd lost sight of who I was, of what my opinions were and what I thought about things. Everything was always about David. The counsellor did make me think of my own values and the reasons why my self-worth had been trashed so heavily by the man who was supposed to love me - and following these sessions I felt empowered for a little while. But this soon wore off as David wore me down, the cycle of abuse then forgiveness, abuse then forgiveness - it just made everything else pale into insignificance.

I'd not attended church as much as I had before meeting David. He didn't understand why I would possibly want to go to church so it had been easier and avoided an argument to just stay home. If I'm truthful, David was like an addiction; the good times between us were good and I craved love like a drug addict craved a high. Despite David beating me, spending all my hard-earned money, despite the possibility that he never truly loved me, all I could think about was saving him. When we'd had a row, this urge - this addiction - saw me drive over to his mum's in my nightie at two o'clock in the morning to try and fix things, even though I needed to be up for work only a few hours later. I once ended up taking a wrong turn right into the middle of where road contractors were working - that's how much grip this addiction had taken hold of me and how far my mind was from reality. Everything was about him. I'd lost 'me'.

David had played on this, calling me "mental" when we were together, feeding my paranoia if he was in a bad mood. He said I was "fucked up in the head". It was never what he'd done, everything was my fault.

"Look what you made me do," was another favourite line when he'd hit me or something had gone wrong.

David was obsessive about cleanliness; his cars had to be spotless. I couldn't get them dirty or there would be hell to pay. I often felt he thought more of his cars than he ever did about me. That's how I felt to anything in his life - second best, rubbish, worthless. I did everything for him, all the shopping, the housework, whilst running the salon, he never made any attempt to pitch in to our life together. If we ran out of milk, I'd have to be the one to go to the shops for more.

He had so little respect for all women. I wasn't the only one he despised. "Slags," he'd say about any woman in his way. His mates were all mild-mannered blokes he could easily push around - he was a classic bully. The only person that seemed to frighten him was his dad.

My mum would waste no time telling me what a loser he was when I saw her. "He's going to make you pregnant, and it will be a bastard of a child!" she'd snap. It was entirely possible she could have just disliked him, but I think she also understood that someone else had control of me at that point, and that was definitely something she didn't like. Controlling me was her game.

* * * * *

Time passed and we experienced a more stable period in our relationship. Because we were getting along so well and because I believed the cycle of abuse had been broken, we started to talk about having a family. The relationship felt balanced, we'd been a couple for around three years now and both David and I were keen to have a child. It took only a couple of months before I fell pregnant and we were both happy.

I dreaded telling Mum, though. Her ideas and morals were so Victorian that telling her I was pregnant meant admitting what I'd done to make the baby! She had this knack of making me feel dirty which saw me petrified of passing on the news.

"It'll be born a bastard," she spat.

Mum always thought David had another agenda than the façade he portrayed. She didn't show that she knew about the abuse as I hid any bruises under long-sleeved tops and put on a good show of unity when visiting.

I was good at parking my troubles at the door, and had done this many times in the salon after a night of terror at David's hands. Whenever I visited Mum we rarely talked about David. Mum still went on about Richard; around this time he'd started to drink heavily and had smashed a car up. Mum told me pointedly that this was my fault. I'd "messed him up and pushed him to do it."

Mum and David were hardly ever together in the same room, and if they were, I could never relax. I thought I always should be someone else, not myself - whoever I was. David and I once planned a Laser Quest session but because my mum's voice in my head was saying over and over, "Grow up!" I felt like I shouldn't go. I did go in the end but I wouldn't fully participate with the others when they were rolling on the floor like children. I also felt as if I should tell her we'd been; it wasn't as if she needed to know - I was a grown woman - it's just that I felt this overwhelming urge to say, even though I knew it would invite ridicule.

David's mum treated me quite well but she was very manipulative - a quality I recognised in my own mother. She'd paint such a helpless picture of events that David dropped everything to be there for her, yet the next minute he was abusing her too.

It was David's mum's idea that we should get married. I thought it was a wonderful way to show David how much I loved him and even he thought it might change him, that marriage might make him grow up.

I wanted to get married in God's eyes. This was different to when I'd married Richard - this time I wanted to do it. I loved him and wanted to acknowledge this properly in church, not in some registry office. I wanted our child to have a proper, respectable grounding in life.

My mum and dad didn't attend the wedding, she said they were too busy. She hated that she couldn't stop it taking place and even made sure the twins didn't come either. I wasn't upset, though I had hoped the twins would come and defy her, but this day was just about David and I, so in the end, David's sister and one of my valued members of staff were in attendance.

After the ceremony, we went back to David's mother's for a buffet. It was a nice day and we both enjoyed it. It felt significant, as if being married had changed things. Things settled down, at least for a few months, and we were genuinely happy and as 'normal' as we ever managed.

Towards the later stages of my pregnancy I was truly worn out. I was still doing mad hours at the salon and although David insisted I let him know when I locked up and left so that he knew when to expect his tea, this particular night I'd forgot to switch my mobile back on (I discouraged him from phoning me at work, blaming the busy turnover of clients, but I just felt I needed one place where I could completely switch off from home life). I walked in the door and got to the bathroom before he yelled, "Where the fuck have you been? Why haven't you got your phone switched on?"

Because I hadn't actually realised my phone was off, I got it out of my bag to check. David snatched the phone from me and threw it in the bathtub, smashing it into pieces. He was so angry, and so the walking on eggshells started again.

David never came to any of the antenatal appointments - he didn't think it was manly. He'd lost interest at this point and seemed to be disgusted at the way my body was changing.

"Fat bitch. Cow arse," he'd sneer.

My hormones were racing and I just felt so low. He was still going out a lot and spent hours on the canopy sunbed we had. One time, as he was going out, I noticed his wedding ring in the bathroom. When I asked him why he'd taken it off he said he didn't want to get a white line on his finger; I just thought, why would this matter if you never intend taking your ring off? He got angry when I questioned him further which played to my insecurities.

I went to call my mother around this time and when I picked the phone up to dial I heard David's voice on the extension. I questioned who he was calling and he ripped the phone off the wall, calling me "fucking paranoid".

He never told me to take it easy all through my pregnancy and watched me work 40-50 hours a week as well as running the house.

When I was eight months pregnant, a colleague of David's was getting married and we were both invited. David didn't seem to want me to go - I felt he was embarrassed with how I looked, or worse still, seeing someone else who would be there. He left on his own but I turned up to the venue a little later to find him sat with a secretary at his firm, his arm round her. He was shocked to see me but I was angry too. He tried to turn things onto me, saying, "What are you doing here?" and when I mentioned what I'd seen, he'd said, "You're seeing things."

I went home on my own and as David blamed me for the row he went to his mum's that night. The next day he was back, saying he was sorry.

The baby was due on December 8th but our son arrived early, on November 19th. The day before the birth I'd still been working full-time in the salon, now desperate to clear debts run up on David's bikes and cars, mortgage and bills - he'd even gone and bought a Porsche. I never spent money on myself and certainly didn't have time to go shopping as I was always working to earn the money; it was even a struggle to find the time to buy what the baby needed. David never mentioned our finances but I always felt that I was the one who should provide for the both of us, and the baby.

I think this urge to provide stems from never feeling good enough. I would hope that, "if I buy this, pay for that, he'll love me. If I help Mum, she'll appreciate me, she'll love me too". It was lost on me that this should have been unnecessary to earn either Mum's or David's affection.

By chance, Mum was helping me out in the salon that last day. She loved being there, probably from when she'd had to give up the greengrocer shop after the twins and I came along. It made her feel important and I know for sure that the success of my business and anything positive I achieved in my career made her proud - well, inwardly, because she'd never say so.

Even though I was three weeks from my due date, when I started to feel warm and flustered I didn't immediately think I was in labour. I actually felt bad about my client as I was forced to sit down and catch my breath. Mum got some cool towels and placed them on my wrists and forehead. I still didn't have a clue what was going on. I clung on to the chair for a little bit while the funny sensation passed then got back to my client. I was still at the salon at 8pm.

It was 9.15pm by the time I dropped Mum off and I still felt strange. I was greeted by David's anger because I was late.

"Where's my tea?" he asked.

I knelt down with my head against our bed.

"I feel poorly. I need to go to bed."

"Fucking drama queen. Where's my tea?"

It was just easier to get back up and make it, which is what I did. As soon as I'd handed him his meal, I went to bed.

My waters broke at 5am the next morning. David was asleep while the fluid gushed from me, he didn't even stir. All I could think about was, "What about my clients at work?"

It was snowing outside and I noticed that the water coming from me was black. The midwife had told us what this meant so I woke David and told him I needed to go to hospital immediately. His reaction was, "Yes! A day off work."

I was worried about getting clean towels to the salon as they'd need them for the day ahead, but I got my labour bag and we set off for the hospital. I was still fretting about everyone else and those damn towels all the way there. David didn't rush, dawdled if anything, with no concern as to whether I was in pain or not. He continued to be oblivious in the delivery room, sat all suave and tanned watching a television show about cheating partners as I laboured away. I nattered so much about the towels that David ended up taking them to the salon - as an excuse to get out of the way, I think. It was actually a relief when he went. He was so unconcerned and uninterested it was upsetting me.

I actually yearned for my mum to be with me; she didn't come until after the baby arrived but she did phone the hospital a few times to check on my progress. David made it back to see his son born and he played the proud father, showing the baby off to everyone as if he'd given birth! *So macho, having a son - a sign of his virility!*

He never once asked how I was, or how painful or hard I'd found labour. Due to the baby's delivery, I'd needed 20-30 stitches. David had already left by this time, and to this day I don't know where he'd actually gone, or how long for - I just remember that he wasn't around.

The snow stopped people coming that day but Mum and my sister came the day after to see the baby. I was concerned about the salon, as I knew from past experience that they were barely capable of things in my absence; one member of staff once rang me on holiday to ask if they could have some money from the till to buy some milk. I used to wonder in sheer disbelief at how none of them could think for themselves; they'd be ringing about stock, wages, etc. even while I was in hospital.

One thing that actually touched me was a letter

from my mum. She passed it to me when I was in hospital, and although it was written in quite a formal way, it told me not to worry about the business and that everything would be okay. I was absolutely shocked; it was so out of character.

I named my son Jordan. I wanted a name that would mean something and felt it should be one from the bible. I named him after the River of Jordan.

Mum seemed quite taken with him, despite being a lifetime hater of children. She was obsessed about his head; said his was 'perfect'. She had a thing about people's heads; she had nicknames about people she met: Snake-head, Bullet-head, Hen-head…it was the first thing she noticed. I was a little surprised at how much she cooed over Jordan, and how nice she was to me at that time. Because she was a man's woman, I think she was also pleased it was a boy - in fact, everyone seemed to have this thought. To David, it was a macho thing but I was happy as I wanted to know how men saw the world, even though it would be years before my son could enlighten me.

I came out of hospital after a couple of days and both David and I were nervous about taking care of this fragile little person. No one showed us what to do with him, so when David tried putting the car seat into the car and it wasn't straightforward his temper started to flare.

I cried all the way home. Was it my hormones? I'd not suffered in pregnancy with morning sickness or cravings - I hadn't had the time to suffer from anything - and I'd never had hormonal trouble before. It bothered me greatly that David didn't seem concerned that I'd just given birth to our child. I'd hoped he'd want to take care of us, but instead I had him swearing at me.

I had to get myself and Jordan out of the car, David never offered to help. I was optimistic that he still could change, but perhaps it was clear even then that he never would.

Chapter Four:
The merry-go-round starts, and it doesn't stop until you get off

It doesn't take a genius to work out what impact a newborn baby would have to a relationship already fractious. The stress of sleepless nights and constant crying can damage the strongest bond and the calmest of personalities, so the recipe for what would follow when we got home from hospital was all there.

Jordan had bad colic that, as any parent knows, causes crying bouts that can last for hours. He never slept but wailed in discomfort continually. I tried my best, as any mother would, to console him and keep him from disturbing his father's sleep. I faced returning to work three weeks after the birth to keep our heads above water financially, which affected the bonding process with my son. There's little wonder I couldn't soothe him when he was in pain. I was bottle-feeding Jordan as I knew returning to work wasn't far away at all, but only skin-to-skin contact worked to calm the baby, which didn't leave me time to fawn over David.

"Shut that fucking kid up, I've got to go to work," he'd shout when Jordan was up in the night.

He took his temper out on me many times in those early weeks, and even Jordan got the heavy-handed treatment too. I'd be dragged out of bed by the hair and told to "see to him", or thrown against the door of the dining room while Jordan was dragged round the side of the bed in his Moses basket - just so we were both out of David's way and he could get his precious sleep. It became easier for me to sleep on the floor so that I could calm the baby before he had chance to scream the place down.

The louder Jordan cried, the worse David's temper was. I was so weak from physical exhaustion; I'd not fully regained my strength from Jordan's labour and knew that full-time work was going to make things so much harder. A few nights before I was back at the salon, Jordan was crying even harder and louder than ever.

"You *will* shut that fucking child up!" David screamed at me. I don't remember what words I said but I tried to stop him from hurting either of us. David kicked out at me, as hard as he could, between my legs. My stitches hadn't fully healed and the force of his kick caused them to open. The pain literally took my breath away.

I recoiled to see David take a wooden rolling pin from the kitchen drawer which he then brought down with force on my head.

"Jordan's ruined my life!" he spat. This wounded me far more than his physical blows and I began crying so hard I could barely breathe. I was so tired and was in severe pain, both physically and emotionally. I remember thinking, "I can't believe the way I'm being treated when all I want is for someone to look after me and Jordan." I had so much work and toil ahead of me at the salon and with a newborn baby to look after too, it's a wonder I didn't just give up there and then.

David stormed off to his Mum's because "he needed to sleep".

I was too embarrassed to go to hospital about the stitches so they were forced to heal themselves.

David didn't return for a few days. He didn't try and see if Jordan or I were okay in the meantime either.

When he did come back nothing was said. That next weekend my sister brought Mum over to visit. Julie was absolutely disgusted to see me cooking David's breakfast while he had a lay-in, with a newborn baby to look after and a return to the salon imminent.

"Sit down, Jayne," she ordered. Whilst I was glad from a physical point of view that someone had taken over, I was embarrassed that she'd seen just what a waste of space David was. I'd always tried to paint a perfect picture of my life behind closed doors. I'd tried to pretend we were just like any other couple or family.

Of course, Mum revelled in the fact that David was so uncaring and uninterested, it proved her point. I felt uncomfortable, not at being proved wrong as such, but for disappointing her.

Julie made me go lay down to get some rest. This made David storm out which worried me. Would he think I'd invited them both over? I couldn't relax because I was so worried he'd be angry when he came back.

He shouted and blamed me when he returned; he didn't like Mum because he could tell she'd got measure of what he was like. He'd told me never to invite her round to the house because he didn't want her there, which is why I'd always gone to see her. Julie bringing Mum that day was completely her decision but he wouldn't listen.

Before long I returned to work and managed to run the house, do the shopping and take care of Jordan too. It was obvious to me that I had strength as there was no question I wouldn't be able to graft or cope with the physical burden, but mentally, I was weaker than ever.

When Jordan was six months old, we were invited by a friend of David's to his wedding. Because of the location, we were staying at David's mother's after the do. David had his friends round him as he got drunk. I was ignored and left to look after Jordan. I wasn't much of a drinker and didn't mind this but after the evening reception they all wanted to go for an Indian meal and I just wanted to go back to his mum's with Jordan as I was tired.

I said to David I'd make my own way to his mum's and he could continue to party but he went ballistic. He dragged me outside and threw me over the bonnet of the car before opening the car door and throwing Jordan, strapped into his car seat, inside. It was dusk and we were out of the way of the revellers, not that David would have cared if we'd been seen. Jordan was crying; David opened the passenger door so violently, the hinges nearly came away. He smashed the car's dashboard with his feet, intent on damage. I was still outside the car trying to calm him down as I was worried what he might do to Jordan.

"How would it look if I went on my own?" he shouted.

By the time we got back to his mum's his temper had flared even more. He dragged me out of the car by my hair into the house whilst his mum looked on. She didn't dare move, she knew how bad his temper could be.

He dragged me by the same method into the bedroom and threw me, then Jordan, onto the double bed. There was a hi-fi cabinet with a large glass door in the room and he ripped the glass front completely off, holding it over me and threatening to smash it on my head.

I was absolutely petrified, screaming and crying to his mum for help but she never came near. Although I'd seen him lose it many times, whether alcohol made a difference, I'd not seen him this angry before. When you hear people say they're 'frothing at the mouth' he literally was. He was like a rabid dog.

I managed to escape from under the glass door and got to the top of the stairs before he caught up with me. He threw me down the whole flight and I landed at the bottom.

His mum found her feet then and stepped over my body to get Jordan who was still screaming upstairs. I genuinely thought at that moment he was going to kill me.

When his mum appeared holding Jordan, I pleaded with her to hand him to me.

"He's alright, leave him here," she begged.

"Please, phone the police," I cried, but she just stood there. "Aren't you going to help me?" I screamed.

"You are his wife," she said. It was as if she

condoned his behaviour, or thought I should accept it because we were married.

I snatched Jordan and ran for my life. I just managed to get both the baby and I in the car when David caught us up.

"Fucking slag!" he shouted, then he spat at me.

He was trying to get into the car but I'd managed to lock it. It didn't stop him buckling the metal as he frantically tried to get to me again.

It was a 40 minute drive home and I was in an absolute state. I was still terrified he was behind us, or that he'd be able to get to me in the house. I phoned the police when I got home, I was so frightened.

I couldn't sleep. David had crossed a line this time, I thought. Jordan had seen it all. That had also been the worst, the angriest, I'd ever seen David. I had money problems with the debts piling up, all from the things he'd bought in my name, I was under pressure trying to make the business a success and working all hours - I just couldn't believe how hard my life was. David didn't care, he could just walk away from everything and return to his charmed life.

The police came the next day and asked if I wanted to make a complaint, which I did. They took the incident seriously and were sympathetic. So that I could go to work, I made an hour's round trip to Julie's who had Jordan for me each day. He still wasn't sleeping through the night, so with my exhaustion from travelling and long hours in the salon, I was dead on my feet.

David stayed at his mum's for a few weeks before coming home. He phoned me in the meantime to trot out the usual words of apology which often turned into heated conversations, as I tried to make him understand what he'd done and how I saw things. He just blamed me for getting him so angry.

I didn't have the strength to argue or the fight to

block his return home. He came back on a casual basis, for sex mainly, before leaving again. I still thought things could work out and thought that if I gave him what he wanted, he might realise how much he loved me.

I think the reality and pain of the situation and how bad things were in my life were so raw that I was unable to think straight. For a few weeks I just went through the motions and tried to carry on as if everything was normal.

At nine months old, Jordan was still up and crying in the night and I was still being tipped out of my bed by David to see to the baby. He'd say, yet again, that he couldn't take it and he'd go back to him mum's for a few nights before returning. I remember thinking at that point that things couldn't carry on this way.

I went to church one Sunday around this time. The sermon was delivered by an elderly lady and every word she spoke seemed to speak directly to me. The message was about destructive relationships and it went right into my heart. I knew, as the sermon said, that I didn't need to put up with things. I'd not been to church for a while as Jordan and work, not to mention everything with David had kept me busy, but her sermon was a sign - a sign that enough was enough. There and then I made a decision.

I told David that we were done. It didn't take me long to pack his things, he had only his clothes and shoes in our house - everything else, furniture, appliances, gadgets, had all been bought and paid for by me. David didn't react which made me nervous. Everyone suggested David shouldn't see Jordan alone so the issue of access to his son worried me too.

Not long after David moved out he came to see me. Jordan was crawling at this stage and we inevitably ended up rowing. I can't be sure it was an accident, but regardless, during the altercation Jordan was hit in the face by David's knee as he pushed him to get out of the way. Jordan understandably started to cry and I instinctively went to pick him up. The red mist descended on David again and he punched his fist into the door (which all had holes in anyway, from previous encounters). I ran from the house with Jordan, crying, and got to the public phone box nearby. I called my mum and dad's house but they weren't in and I got the answering machine. I was terrified David had followed me out of the house so all the machine recorded was Jordan's scream and my cries of help.

I didn't dare return home at first in case David was still there but after nearly an hour I tentatively went back. David had gone.

Unbeknown to me, my dad had rung David's mum's house after getting the answer-machine message, wanting to find out what had happened.

Out of character, my dad demanded, "Where's my fucking daughter and grandson?"

David was already there, and shouted down the phone that he was going to kill my dad.

"Bully! Come and try it!" Dad said, before slamming the phone down.

David's mum's was about an hour's drive away from my parents'. Later that afternoon, my mum was on the phone to my sister when she saw David pull up in a car with his sister. Mum immediately put the phone down and called the police.

My dad was of a stocky build but his age was against him and David beat him up quite badly, breaking two of his ribs and blacking his eyes. Dad didn't want David in the house because he feared he'd smash everything up. David picked up a wooden garden bench and threw it at my father then went on to buckle the porch door as he tried to get in the house. My dad did his best to stop him in the process and tried to give as good as he got.

David's sister got hold of Mum who responded by swinging her walking stick, catching the girl's hair which became entwined. As they struggled, a clump of her ponytail came away in Mum's hand.

Julie turned up just before the police and she started on David when she saw what he'd done to Dad. I was still completely unaware of all this, at home with Jordan.

The police handcuffed David and pinned his sister to the ground. They bundled him into their vehicle and made his sister follow in her car. They asked Mum and Dad if they wanted to press charges but they declined. The police made sure an injunction was put in place which banned David from coming near Jordan. They also admitted they'd never seen anyone drive in such a temper for over an hour without their anger diffusing or subsiding. It came as no surprise to anyone that they recommended he receive anger management counselling.

A couple of hours after I'd argued with David I remembered the answer-machine message and made my way over to Mum's to tell her what had gone on in our house. I was absolutely shocked and upset at the sight of Dad's swollen face and the damage David had caused. I remember thinking, "There's no going back now".

The incident prompted many questions from my family about what had gone on in our home behind closed doors. When I told them of the things David had done, none of them could believe I'd hidden it for so long. Julie even suggested David was schizophrenic.

"I wouldn't have let a man hit me," Mum said. She couldn't resist adding, "You should have stayed with Richard."

She seemed relieved that Jordan was safe now, though the same concern didn't seem to stretch to my wellbeing. She even hovered over the subject of whether she should take care of Jordan, insinuating I was incapable of looking after him.

Mum and Dad were glad David was off the scene now. "If he ever comes near us ever again, I'll fucking shoot him," she warned.

* * * * *

David left us alone after that. I was on my own for the next couple of years and pined for him, heartbroken that things didn't work out. I couldn't switch my feelings off nor forget about the good times we'd enjoyed, however sparse they'd been. Even though I knew what he'd done to all of us was wrong, I still waited for him to come back. I still thought I could rescue him from his cycle of abuse.

My faith had taught me that people could change and seek redemption. The bible preached that we were all capable of transformation. I didn't want to go back to how things were but I was hurt that he'd never showed he cared about me or Jordan. He left me to struggle with raising our child on my own; however he felt about me, he would have known how hard things were financially. Was it too much to think that he'd realise this and leave us a pack of nappies or some food on the doorstep? He could have phoned or left a card to see how we were but it was as if he'd dropped from the face of the earth. He didn't care about us, there was no contact.

The debts were really piling pressure on me back then. Red letters and phone calls were coming daily and although the business was earning money, it couldn't produce it fast enough. All the loans were in my name and I had to work my way out of them, which meant my relationship with Jordan was far more distant than I'd have liked. Initially, after David left, we were still living in the house we'd shared which was an hour's drive from Mum's. She'd said she'd look after Jordan while I was at the salon but he was still suffering from colic and therefore up all night. Because of this, he was also feeding in small but frequent amounts which meant I had to give him a bottle in various lay-bys on the way to Mum's. No one had a clue how hard things were for me as I plastered on a front, as usual.

My home phone was cut off and I was warned the gas and electricity were next as I hadn't been able to pay the bills in time. I made sure all the staff at the salon got paid before anything else, but ten days before the cut-off deadline I told Mum and Dad of the situation. They could not believe anyone had hidden something so worrying for so long. By this time, I was numb to the situation. Mum seemed to feel sorry for me but she also seemed to take pleasure from seeing me as a victim.

I was surprised, therefore, at her compassion and the help she gave me at that time. She accompanied me to all the court proceedings; I thought I could end up being sent to prison. This would have frightened anyone but I dealt with it all clinically, as if I was watching the situation happen to someone else. I did take comfort from Mum being with me, though.

I admit, the thought of my business - the salon I'd built up with every fibre of my soul - going under was nothing short of devastating to begin with and it broke my heart. But by the time we got to discussing this eventuality with legal bodies and on form after form, I'd come to terms with the notion and felt very little.

I was told to take out what I needed from the business, physical things like stock, etc. but it felt as if I was pilfering - even though it was still all mine, at least for a little while. Figures drawn up at one consultation showed I'd spent thirty thousand pounds getting the business off the ground and the amount it went for when sold was a lot, lot less than this. At this point it sunk in and I felt sick. As I left the meeting I was crying and felt so weak that I collapsed in the lift. Mum had to bring me back round.

I felt as if my life had been taken from me. My car and house had to be sold off and bailiffs were coming to take my furniture and any possessions I still had. I just felt stupid - stupid that David had taken so much. He'd damaged me physically, emotionally and now his desire to show the trapping of 'his' wealth had taken my business, my livelihood and my home. He'd taken everything he wanted and had just walked away from the situation.

All I'd ever wanted was to be loved.

* * * * *

I'd heard through our village's grapevine that David's dad thought I was suffering from post-natal depression, so even now, everything had to be my fault. There was no shame to be shared by their family.

I came away from the final meeting at the insolvency office with just £15 to my name. It was literally all I had.

I suggested to Mum that we went to The Hilton for dinner.

I still had my dignity. As I sat in The Hilton with Mum no one had a clue how destitute I was. I could still act the part, put on a front.

I thought, "I may have lost everything, but I'm still as good as everyone here."

Dinner came to £10.99.

I came to my senses in the hotel; I was going to pick myself back up again. This was the first step. No one was going to do it for me; I had to take care of myself and Jordan.

That Sunday I returned to church with Jordan crying in my arms. As the collection plate came around I didn't have any money to add. The woman next to me took a £20 note from the plate and pressed it into my hand. I was overcome with the gesture. The whole congregation knew of my troubles and wanted to help.

Although my parents could help out a little, in terms of childcare and a bit of food here and there, they weren't in a position to help me financially. I would have to swallow my pride and go down to the DHSS office.

Having always earned money and been successful in business, I was embarrassed. Applying for any benefits or support was a completely alien experience.

Because I had Jordan to consider too, I went along to the social and was told I had twelve months before I would completely lose the house. This at least gave me some leeway and a place to live whilst I sorted out everything else. I hadn't let the bailiffs take everything; I'd hidden some items up at my sister's before they called, so I wasn't completely stripped. With milk vouchers and family allowance I had just enough to get by, and the extra time at home made such a difference to mine and Jordan's relationship. We started bonding and I played games with him and revelled in being a mother. We did lots of walking together and I joined Priory Campus, a group made up of other mums that had suffered through domestic abuse. I felt as though Jordan and I were finally getting some support.

Although I was fulfilled emotionally and spiritually, financially the twelve month window was looming. I couldn't apply for any credit and I did start to worry what would become of us. Around this time I was also being hassled by my next-door neighbour; he'd come to my window night after night with no top on and holding a bottle of wine. He was married but played on how low I felt and kept asking me to let him in so we could chat. I didn't have the confidence to tell him to get lost at first but after so long I questioned why he was targeting a vulnerable single woman. I felt sure he was just after taking advantage of me so the next night I threatened to tell his wife if he didn't stop coming. He never came again.

I couldn't understand why people wouldn't leave me be. After everything I'd been through, all I wanted was to build a new life with my son.

The landlord who had owned the premises where I'd run my salon offered me a proposition: if I started the business back up, he'd buy my bungalow and I'd pay him rent. He told me he was doing me a favour, and that, "I could do him favours in return". I didn't want to be beholden to a dirty old man who could prey on a desperate single woman so I flatly refused; in fact, the very thought made me so angry. I couldn't believe someone could actually suggest such a thing.

There was little wonder I was so distrustful of men after my experiences, but every one I met seemed to have an agenda. I just wanted to find someone honest and caring. The only men I met like that were in church, and all were married. They were honest and open - a different breed, if you like - and seemed to speak from the heart in a genuine manner. They understood about problems and temptation; I'd have been very happy if I could have found someone this way.

No, I had no one but Jordan. It was him and me against the world. It was no good feeling sorry for myself.

The thing I needed to move forward with my life was some transport. Dad suggested buying a little car on my behalf which I'd pay back to him in instalments. With a car I could find work, and with an income, I could find us somewhere to live as the deadline for our home was fast approaching.

I was banned from setting up in business as part of the insolvency agreement, but my sister, Julie, and her husband set up a new salon in their names. One of my ex-staff ran the salon and I worked there part-time. As soon as word got round that I was working again, all my old customers came flooding in which gave me renewed purpose. It almost felt like a duty to help these women feel good on the inside and out.

Despite this progress and the little car my mum and dad had found, it still broke my heart to lock the door on my home for the last time. The day I left the house I felt such a failure, but I told myself it was just bricks and mortar. I vowed to start again, and that the door I was closing was the one to the past.

My brother-in-law's mum had a little house near my sister that was up for rent, so I took that - literally, as one door closed, another one opened. With the church's support and being so near to family and the new business it seemed as if a new beginning was in-front of me.

Jordan's second birthday was approaching and Mum found me crying one day.

"Don't tell me you're still crying over that bastard!" she sneered.

Whether it was because David didn't seem to care that it was Jordan's birthday or not, or just from all we'd been through at that time, I reflected on everything that had happened and my emotions caught up with me. This got Mum angry for some reason, and she uttered to Dad, "After all we've done for her."

She demanded Dad got his shoes on and they left.

Jordan was going through a clingy stage which piled more pressure on me as we had to play hide and seek every day, just to get him to leave the house. I felt insecure about whether I was doing everything right and Mum stepped in, taking more control. She got a key cut to my house and put new fences up, even though it was a rented property. She basked at being in charge once more and when my sister asked if I could do more hours at the salon, she told her I couldn't. My voice was lost again.

I wanted to send Jordan to a childminding centre so that he could socialise with other children and not be as clingy. I also thought it would allow me to do extra hours and earn a little more money, but Mum came with me to view the centre and that was that.

She pulled everything to pieces and said, "You're not leaving him here. They're torturing these kids."
Despite Jordan being my child, and despite me being 36 years old, I still couldn't stand up to her. So Jordan didn't go to the centre.

* * * * *

As if further evidence was needed of my inability to stand up for myself was needed, I collected yet another weird stalker around this time. The rented house was near a country pub and the chef who worked there had spotted me coming in and out of my house, which backed onto the pub's garden. It was common knowledge with the regulars that this chef was fond of me.

He'd ask me out all the time. Even if I said no, his response was, "But you're single". I felt like a piece of meat up for grabs. He'd knock on my door after finishing work and I'd have to turn the lights off and pretend I wasn't in - every single night!

At one point my underwear went missing from my washing line and I knew who'd taken it; the proximity to the pub meant it wasn't hard for him to get into my garden. I felt a little intimidated after that and kept wondering what I did, or what signals I gave off, that kept attracting these weirdos.

The stalking finished when the chef left his job and the area. I got friendly with the girl next door and she coaxed me to go into the pub now that the chef had left. A guy in the pub, Rick, spotted me in there, and he started asking locals about me. He wasn't my cup of tea, I didn't find him attractive at all, but everyone urged me to give him a chance, saying how nice he was and that looks weren't everything.

I went to a dinner dance with Rick shortly after but I found that looks had to count for something; he made my skin crawl in the same way that Richard used to. I didn't see him after that but this didn't stop him coming round with flowers and presents. I made it clear I wasn't interested, but it was as if he was obsessed about me. He was really pushy and I didn't want to offend him but I felt so frustrated that if I had a day off or went anywhere he'd be there. He'd invite himself in and wouldn't leave. And he'd take over - he'd cook the tea or book tickets somewhere without even asking me. He smothered Jordan with toys but it was clear to me he was just trying to buy my affection. Just another one out to control me. Even Mum called him "a foul bastard".

Eventually, enough was enough and I stood up to him. He got really aggressive and pushed me. I got a bruise on the back of my leg but at least he'd got the message.

The term in the rented house was coming to an end and the owner wanted to sell the property. The car my parents had bought me also needed a new exhaust. I was back to being helpless again and felt no further forward. I'd stowed away from the bailiffs a Gucci watch that I'd bought for myself and an Italian kitchen table; I had to decide which one to sell to pay for what the car needed. I decided on the table as it had meant a lot to me to treat myself to the watch.

I found myself homeless again and had no choice but to go into a refuge. Despite what some may think, I didn't mind this. The refuge felt safe. It was in a secret location for obvious reasons - I was away from my family, and the constant badgering from Rick before he'd left the scene was now gone.

I was so frustrated that I'd allowed things in my life to get out of hand yet again. I'd been left unable to take control and with a mind like cotton wool. When would I put my own needs first?

The break from everything did me good. Mum couldn't come near me for a start. The fact that the refuge was very basic and that none of us there had anything didn't seem to matter. I still managed to get to work and looked forward to the peace of the refuge when I got back. I joined a church and an Alpha Course which helped me cleanse my thoughts and look to the future.

I knew the refuge was a short-term thing, and that I needed to find a house with a permanent or long-term lease. Although I found the refuge restful, I felt unsettled at the uncertainty of mine and Jordan's future - I felt a bit like a gypsy. The refuge's support gave me the space to plan my next steps.

I started researching council houses and housing association properties for something suitable. Long-term, I wanted to be in the same area as my family which meant some considerable searching down suitable streets for vacant houses. I couldn't understand why the other women in the refuge were content to wait for others to help them, instead of getting up and doing something about their situation. It gave me some comfort that at least I was being proactive.

I eventually found a two-bedroom house that was empty, in the area I wanted. It was fairly new and although compact, it looked like a mansion to me! I rang the council as I stood outside and told them of my interest in the property, then prayed and prayed to God that it would become mine.

As I was homeless with a child and classed as vulnerable it was straightforward. Intuition had told me that this property was meant for me; it just felt right. Mum saw it and liked it which was out of character - I think she was even a little jealous. I don't know why, as it was unfurnished and had literally nothing on the inside. I had a 'befriender', a mentor from the refuge who gave me a single bed and two rugs to start off with. I also qualified for a start-up grant which meant I could buy a cooker. I couldn't afford a carpet but we had basic facilities at least. However, my dad wasn't happy about Jordan walking about on bare floorboards so he got the house fully carpeted. I was very grateful and touched that he'd done something so wonderful for me. He'd used the excuse with my mum that Jordan had actually hurt his feet. It was the only way she'd allow my dad to do such a thing.

I bought a used sofa for £100 from my wages and over the next 18 months I managed to completely decorate and furnish the house, though all the furniture and fixings were either second-hand or donated. I got a real sense of pride knowing that I'd finally managed to make a home for me and my son.

Although I felt a sense of achievement it still annoyed me that David had never contributed to Jordan's wellbeing. He'd never paid for any of his things or given me any money for food; after all, Jordan was his child too. I was decorating Jordan's bedroom with some bargain paint and second-hand furniture when I reached a turning point. I was going to be more assertive. I wrote to David at his mum's address and asked for some financial contribution towards his upbringing or I was going to approach the CSA. I didn't hear anything back personally, but a cheque for £60 was posted to my sister's address, and then again each month from then on. There was no letter asking how Jordan was or anything, it appeared that the threat of the CSA was the only catalyst for this action.

Now that I'd got the house looking nice - no one would have walked in and guessed that the contents were from markets or second-hand - I felt proud that I'd got myself back on my feet. Jordan started attending the school over the road and life was actually quite good. The only thing marring things was when my mother visited and I felt I was being judged all over again. I could never rest when she came; she had this knack of making me feel like a young schoolgirl, despite my age.

I'd not been in the house long when I started to feel unwell. I just thought I was under the weather due to stress and the energy spent making the house a home. I lost a lot of weight and decided to go to the doctors to see if he could say what it might be. I was always hungry yet often found myself doubled up with pain. The doctor wasn't interested, though.

"It's just stress. What you young ladies do to lose weight!" he joked.

Not long after my visit to the doctor, I was at home when I felt what I can only describe as my stomach 'snapping'. A wave of acute pain knocked me from my feet and I lay in agony on the kitchen floor.

Jordan came in and was horrified and scared to see me unconscious but luckily, he had the foresight to phone my mum and dad.

Years of abuse, stress and pain had caused an ulcer to grow inside me until it was the size of a fist. That day, the ulcer had burst and septicaemia had set in, perforating my appendix at the same time.

And that's how I found myself drugged up to my eyeballs to block the pain on the eve of the new millennium, when those two women walked past my bed and assumed I was just another pisshead or druggie.

It tests my beliefs sometimes when I see murderers, muggers, rapists and evil people walk the earth with seemingly little recompense, yet my whole life has been full of pain and suffering for nothing more than the need to be loved and cared for. Even now, writing this, and despite my faith in God, I still don't understand the injustice of it all.

* * * * *

I was in hospital for three weeks, and in intensive care for one of those. Mum looked after Jordan for me, which is something I'll always be grateful for. She was actually really good to me at this point. The help I needed was of a practical kind; I couldn't eat or walk when I was eventually discharged so she moved in to help care for me. I really appreciated her help and I think it helped me to see that she did love me, even if she could only show it in a pragmatic way.

She'd wash my hair and cook for me, things like

omelettes and boiled eggs to get my strength up. I was so thin at that point that the stitches in my stomach burst open as there wasn't enough fat cover for the skin to knit together. I would be left screaming in pain as a result.

Mum rubbed my back when I was suffering but she still had to have her say. "You'll meet another bloody man, won't you?" she'd snap, not in the sense that she worried I'd always be alone, but as a warning that the same could happen again with the wrong type of guy (the type she expected I'd choose).

It took a long time, a really long time, before I was back to full strength and able to care for Jordan on my own. Life eventually returned to an even keel and sufficient time had passed from the insolvency episode to now apply for credit. I decided to start up in business again.

I got a credit card, as it was the only way I could fund the start-up, and found a small space suitable for a salon. Dad and I painted it, and again, I made it look nice with second-hand items. My experience in the field of precise budgeting, bartering and hunting down bargains went a long way. I managed to get all my equipment and fit the shop out for three and a half thousand pounds. I sent letters to all my old customers and took the gamble that each one would come back to me and I could cover the rent as a result.

The gamble paid off and the salon was an instant success. I approached an enterprise company for funding; I didn't manage to secure any money but during this process I was introduced to Michelle, who came to work for me part-time. It wasn't long before she became integral to the continued success of the salon.

I'd started from scratch and built a life yet again. I'd been through hell so many times, been physically, emotionally and mentally abused year in, year out, and nearly died on more than one occasion.

Each time, and faced with more adversity than

the average person endures during their whole lifetime, I'd found the strength to carry on, to come back, to find myself. My faith never faltered, the love for all in my life never left and my need to give never diminished.

By now, most people reading would assume I'd had my fair share of grief and heartache, that I'd learned by this time what a destructive relationship looked like and how to listen to my intuition. Because I would, in your shoes.

As you'll find, by reading on, all the warning signs in the world didn't stop me from making the same mistake.

And so the cycle started again....

* * * * *

Chapter Five:
Same cycle, different man...

Michelle became a huge support in my life at this point. I look back now and see that I had no problem attracting strong women around me who became soul-mates and great confidantes - why the same couldn't apply to the men in my life, only God knows.

Michelle had been through a similar relationship to the one I'd endured with David, so she understood my lack of self-esteem and how low the relationship had left me. She helped to build my confidence slowly. Eventually we went out into the local town for a drink; the last thing on my mind was another relationship, I promise you, but I admit it was a distraction to join the human race.

One particular Bank Holiday weekend Michelle was insistent that we went out. I truly wasn't all that bothered but she begged and pleaded until I was worn down. I thought so little of the night out that I didn't even bother to get changed. As we were in one venue, having a dance, we noticed a group of men leering and ogling. I didn't like their goading and certainly didn't feel flattered that they were directing their drunken appreciation towards Michelle and I, it made me feel uneasy. One of the group came over to us and thrust a business card in my hand, explaining it wasn't his but his friend's. Two thoughts sprang to mind: Why would anyone come for a night out with their business card? And why didn't the guy in question have the nerve to give it to me himself?

I didn't go over to the group; instead, we finished our drinks in peace before leaving for another pub. After this one, we headed back to the previous club to carry on dancing.

The same 'friend' came over once more. "Will you go and talk to this guy? He finds you attractive."

I looked across to the man in question and the only thing that I really noticed was his very bald head. (Perhaps a habit passed on from my mother?) He was so hairless that I initially thought he was ill, that he must have leukaemia or something. He appeared to have muscles on muscles, which isn't my type at all - he was very pumped up indeed.

Michelle was egging me on to go talk to him, so dutifully, I went over. We started chatting and found we had the same surname which immediately gave us common ground. I wasn't over-enthusiastic by any means. I wasn't ready for a relationship and I therefore didn't want to encourage this guy, whose business card gave his first name as Martin. It seemed a brief conversation before I returned to Michelle, but little did I realise how much information he'd gleaned from me in those few minutes. He hadn't asked direct questions and I never felt pressed to divulge anything, but at that point, I had no idea just how skilled this man was at manipulation.

One thing I did ask was why he carried a business card when he was drinking with his friends, saying it seemed unusual. He replied that it was coincidence, that the cards had just happened to be in his pocket. He pressed me to ring him but I gave no promises and actually tore up his card on the way home, throwing it out of the taxi window. I had no intention of ringing him, and neither had he made a huge impression on me.

The next day was the Bank Holiday so the salon was closed. On the Tuesday morning I went to open up as usual and found a business card had been posted through the letterbox. It was Martin's card sat staring at me from the mat. I picked up the card, puzzling how he'd known where my salon was, to see the words, "Some things are worth chasing".

My first emotion was flattery; how much must he have liked me to go to such lengths? Immediately after this thought was a feeling of panic - what other information had I unwittingly given him? The thought he'd been in this part of the town and to my salon door was unsettling. For the second time, I threw his card away.

On the Thursday morning of that same week I had flowers delivered to the salon, with Martin's card attached. It said exactly the same thing on the back - "Some things are worth chasing".

My staff couldn't fail to notice the flowers and asked who sent them. Michelle was still egging me on to ring him.

"He's more your type, Michelle," I said. He certainly wasn't mine.

"What have you got to lose?" she asked.

Now there's not one of you who won't realise by now how naively I look at some situations. I thought, through politeness more than anything, that I should text Martin to thank him for the flowers. Not being technologically minded either, I managed to give him my mobile number by doing so. As soon as I realised this I chided myself. I'd left the gate open.

That was that. Texts and calls bombarded me. So as not to disrupt my business or affect the service I gave to my clients, I kept my phone on silent while at the salon. In one afternoon alone I'd received twenty missed calls and texts from him.

I answered a couple, trying my best to play down his attention. I still didn't think him attractive - in fact, he actually sounded gay on the phone; his voice was quite high-pitched and effeminate for someone so outwardly macho. It didn't seem to make much difference if I rebutted his requests to take me out or if I ignored his calls, he just would not take the hint.

Mum and my brother got wind of what was happening which gave them fodder to comment. Mum would mutter, "the bloody men you choose!". She didn't understand that I hadn't exactly chosen him. I held him at arm's length for quite a while before I finally gave in and agreed to meet up. My stipulation, or stab at some control, was that I'd go out with him for a couple of hours only - making the excuse that I wasn't used to being away from Jordan for long periods of time. I told Martin to pick me up at 6pm, but that I had to be back for 8.30pm. These boundaries on my time were my way of keeping a distance between us.

I can't lie, when we were out Martin was very charming. He said all the things a woman would want to hear. He was so forward with his flattery that my mind began to question whether beauty was only skin deep, and why we only ever seem to go for people's looks. I felt older and wiser than I had at the outset of my relationship with David and thought no man would put me in the same position again. I'd lived through his abuse so vividly that the signs were imprinted on my brain.

Whereas David seemed child-like, Martin appeared emotionally mature, opening up that night to his past as a stripper. He told of the stress this life had given him which had caused him to develop alopecia. His frankness was something I completely admired, and I was further flattered that he'd chosen to share his experiences with me.

He also told me of his depression, and of how his somewhat seedy sideline had only existed to pay him through college.

"I want you to know about everything, rather than hear it from someone else," he said.

In his stripping days he'd formed a group which had been quite successful, touring our area and further afield. He'd been the lead guy and his 'pumped up' exterior stemmed from wanting to look good when stripping on stage. His agent, he went on to say, was a drag queen and on top of being a stripper he'd offered escort services too. Though he seemed to share this information willingly, with the hint that all this was in the past, I found out later that he was still stripping in those early days of our relationship.

In return, I opened up to Martin about my relationship with David. I didn't think about how he was storing this information, and what impression he was forming of me as a result, though it seems obvious now. I told him about how David had left me in debt and how subsequent bankruptcy meant I lost everything. He listened intently as I described how I got back on my feet from the abyss that is rock bottom. How this played into his hands, I couldn't have dreamt at that point - I just thought this was part of the chivalrous attitude he was displaying.

Manipulation goes through many different stages; firstly, trust has to be established. By opening up, Martin had given me the feeling he trusted me with his life story, and there was no reason for me to think he'd behave any differently with the information I was innocently feeding him.

I genuinely took his interest in me to be an indication of how much he liked me. That night, he wined and dined me, listened to every word I spoke and said all the things any woman would want to hear. He held doors open for me like a true gentleman and held my hand across the table. Nothing was too much trouble for him and it would have been obvious to all how keen he was.

After everything I'd been through with David and due to the time I'd spent single I felt healed, wiser and in tune with my internal voice. I'd vowed, when David and I had split, that I'd never go near another man like that for as long as I lived. I trusted that I'd know the type of man who would prove to be bad news, should I come across one.

But here, in front of me, was a man seemingly mature, respectful, appreciative, courteous and gentle. He took me home after our first 'date' and didn't push to come in, asking only for the chance to take me out again. I'd enjoyed the evening but I still didn't feel any attraction towards him, so I didn't give him a firm answer.

This lack of interest I displayed didn't put Martin off; he continued to beg for another chance to see me again. I'd planned to go for a drink with Michelle soon afterwards and he volunteered to take us into town so that we wouldn't need to order a taxi, to which I agreed. He picked us both up as he said he would and dropped us in town then said he would meet us later in one of the pubs. We didn't see hide nor hair of him for the rest of the evening.

When he next got in touch I asked him why he'd not met up with us.

"I didn't have any money," he said.

Alarm bells started to ring. He'd the money for flowers, meals and his image. I couldn't put my finger on what my intuition was telling me or flagging up, but my faith kicked in before I could listen to my inner voice.

"Smooth words may hide a wicked heart, just as a pretty glaze covers a common clay pot" **Proverbs 26:33**

As Christians, we're taught not to judge a book by its cover or jump to conclusions, so I resolved to 'park' whatever it was I felt until I knew more.

The next time I saw Martin, he'd invited me to his home where he lived alone. I went with curiosity. Although the street and area lived up to his impeccable image, I was shocked to see his home severely neglected. His garden was overgrown, there were stains on his carpet and the place was an absolute tip. Martin didn't seem phased that the house was in such a mess as he made no excuse to why it looked the way it did.

I was absolutely bewildered. "When was the last time you did the garden?" I asked him.

He just shrugged and said he had no drive to do it, that his depression sapped his energy.

I heard myself say, "Have you got any cleaning stuff and a vac?"

When he nodded, I said, "Do you want me to come

this weekend and clean up?"

Of course, he said yes.

I found out that he was claiming incapacity benefit for his depression, although he was doing bits of work on the side. He gave me a spare key to the house so that I could let myself in to clean. I turned up the following weekend, and walked from room to room, desperately wondering where to start.

There was no order whatsoever to the house and there were wires and plugs everywhere. I did what I could but I was limited to where I could clean and tidy, the place was in such disorder. I'd even brought with me a salmon salad, plating it up for him to eat when he got back. I remember thinking, "this guy needs looking after".

He had eggs in his fridge so out of date they'd turned green. There were small bottles of medication in there too but I had no clue as to what they were for. Martin had said he often had friends staying over but it was obvious from the house that it was more a communal 'doss-down' place. There were beds and mattresses everywhere - squeezed into every space available. He'd also told me he used to rent rooms out. This puzzled me; couldn't he afford to live there?

As I cleaned I came across a few white plastic pots with screw-top lids in a cupboard, amongst yet another mass of wires. I unscrewed one and saw what appeared to be small white rocks and powder. In another I found a green, clay-like substance and a third stored pills of some kind. There were also bottles of lighter fluid, tin foil and loads of matches everywhere which again puzzled me, as he wasn't a smoker. I wondered why he had these things in his house - it's easy to see these as signs when looking back but I'm inherently trusting of everyone I meet.

I admit I'm not the most street-wise person around, in fact, I'd say I was then decidedly naïve. I didn't know that what I'd found were hard drugs, that the white rocks were cocaine and the green clay was heroin - I'd actually thought the pills were some type of vitamin! It turns out these were amphetamines (speed). No, nothing flagged up to me at all at that point.

I also noticed lady's clothes in Martin's wardrobe which I assumed were from an old girlfriend, and when vacuuming under his bed I found a strange pump. I was so clueless to what this could have been that I just put it back where I found it. I had absolutely no idea that the pump was actually an enhancer that Martin used to enlarge his penis before going on stage to strip.

Also under his bed was a white box. Inside was a black bag containing diaries and information on his stripping gigs. There was far more detail in that box than what he'd told me. Alongside these diaries was a host of accessories like baby oil, vibrators and porn videos. Whether it stemmed from my mother's Victorian views on the whole world of sex, things like this weren't everyday objects to me.

Two things I did find particularly strange in the house was an orange plug and wire that led into the attic space and what seemed like an office chair at the top of the stairs. The chair, I later found out, Martin and his pals would use in bondage play.

I cleaned and tidied the house as best I could before Martin came home. He thought the house looked great, calling me 'wife material' and asking me where I'd been all his life. I asked him, in total innocence, about the pump under his bed.

"It's a cock pump," he said, demonstrating graphically how he placed bands on the bottom of his penis so that it remained enlarged during shows. He showed no embarrassment or awkwardness - this was truly a well used and everyday object to him.

I wasn't sure what to think. I had started to see beyond Martin's physical appearance and what he'd showed me was a sensitive personality; what I'd found that day didn't seem to sit with that. I left, still reserving judgement.

Martin called and texted me just as much, if not more so, once he'd seen how well I could look after him. He kept insisting on coming to my house once Jordan was in bed. I tentatively introduced them in those early days and Jordan took an instant dislike to Martin. He was six by this point and for the whole of his life that he remembered, I'd been the mainstay. There'd been no father figure other than my dad and brother; it had been just the two of us against the world. It wasn't a surprise that he failed to welcome this man. I just took it that he was simply jealous but I look back now and wonder if he'd picked up on vibes I was oblivious to.

In those early days, as I got to know Martin more, he encouraged me to meet his circle of friends. We went along to one of their houses for some celebration or other and I spent a little time talking to one of Martin's male friends. I was only mingling, trying to be friendly, I wasn't particularly interested in this guy. In-front of everyone, Martin told me to tone it down.

"You're getting too friendly," he warned.

I was dumbstruck. I said I didn't know what he was on about.

"Go on, fuck off with him!" he shouted as he stormed out of the house in a foul rage.

I was mortified and his friend was equally embarrassed. I left to go home and just thought his jealousy was stupid. I gave Martin the benefit of the doubt - if I'd have had any inkling of what was to come I'd have ended it there and then. The next day he said he was sorry, he didn't know what had come over him. I dismissed the incident easily - too easily - and continued to believe Martin was someone who would treat me well.

Every time Martin rang me at home Jordan created.

I remember once answering the phone to him in the loo with the door locked, Jordan banging and screaming on the other side. Martin tried harder to get on with him at first and we planned a trip to The Deep in Hull. All day Jordan played up and I heard Martin call him, "a little bastard".

Looking back, I should have stuck up for Jordan but I was just embarrassed about my son's behaviour. Martin soon stopped trying to befriend him and just concentrated on increasing the time when we could be on our own. He saw that my parents helped out a lot with Jordan and encouraged me to ask them for more babysitting.

After a couple of months, Martin suggested a holiday in Cyprus, for the two of us. He made it clear that Jordan wasn't expected to come along, so I asked Mum if she'd look after him, saying to her that the trip was a chance for Martin and I to have some time alone. Mum had met Martin by this point, but thought he was "a foul bastard" and that he was only interested in sex.

"Who'd want to lay under that?" she'd say, "I don't know what you see in him."

Mum agreed to look after Jordan, regardless. The holiday itself, I had to pay for, as Martin said he didn't have much money. Knowing he was on benefits, I didn't think much of it and we flew off.

The first half of the week was fine but half-way through, Martin seemed uneasy. He'd pace up and down the apartment and appeared really anxious - he was like a different person. He either wanted to get away from me or sleep the whole time; I thought it must have been me that caused him to feel like that. I felt uneasy again.

One day I mentioned the orange plug in his house that led to the attic and he said he grew cannabis. It was the first time he'd mentioned drugs. He said the plants were ready for cropping and that they'd be worth some money but he was worried about the smell they gave off and that they'd need watering in his absence. He rang his mum from

Cyprus and told them to go water the cannabis plants. I expected they'd go ballistic but they didn't seem perturbed at all - they went round and watered them.

I told Martin that this all had to stop if we were to be in a relationship - the mates he hung around with who were a bad influence and the cannabis plants had to go from the house. Initially he tried to persuade me that his friends weren't bad but I wasn't convinced. I've always believed 'bad company corrupts good character' (**Corinthians 15:33**).

"Don't let the errors of evil people lead you down the wrong path and make you lose your balance." **Peter 3:17**

Finally, he agreed, saying he'd do it "for me". When he seemed to want the relationship to work, I thought I'd finally found the type of love I craved. Our relationship wasn't perfect - whose was? Martin loved me enough to want to change his life.

I even approached his mum at this point, to ask for support. She told me he'd been on drugs since he was 15. What shocked me was her easy acceptance of his actions - she said it was easier to accept and ignore than suffer the reactions of other people if they found out!

All this was planned from the start in Martin's mind. The 'sacrifice' he was making was just ammunition he could use against me later in our relationship. The situation had been manipulated so that I believed Martin was equally committed, which saw me finally fall for him hook, line and sinker.

He had me where he needed me.

* * * * * *

It wasn't long after our holiday that Martin invited Jordan and I to move in with him.

"Why rent when you can come and live here?" he'd

say.

My parents thought I was stupid.

"You're crackers!" Mum spat.

But I thought this was the chance of a new life - one where we'd be a family and live happy ever after. I'd managed to save some money once I'd got back on my feet and knew I could make Martin's house a home for the three of us. I'd asked him to put Jordan and I before the drugs and the seedier parts of his previous life, which he had - and I took this as a commitment towards the three of us becoming a family unit.

I admit that I had rose-tinted glasses on. Martin's parents seemed just as keen for Jordan and I to move in and even helped me move - stripping my old house like locusts.

I was still attending church at this point but once I moved in with Martin, he questioned my need to keep going. He came with me a couple of times but was so antagonising that I'd wished he'd stayed at home. I was embarrassed when he argued with some of the other church members. You could never win an argument with Martin, he always had to have the last word or upper hand. I also distanced myself from my family a little. I visited them, though not quite as often, but I wouldn't invite my parents over to the house as I was so ashamed of its state.

Once I moved in I found out the true extent to Martin's debt situation. From my own experience following the break-up of my relationship with David and subsequent bankruptcy, I perhaps wasn't as shocked or disgusted as the next person. I knew that even the most well-to-do, decent people could succumb to problems with money.

However, Martin's priorities astonished me. He'd think nothing of spending the mortgage money on a stag do. He had CCJs, a list of them as long as your arm; he'd loads of mobile phones that had all been cut off because he'd not kept up with the payments on each contract, his phone bills were huge - £800, £1,000. He had no landline so I arranged for one to be put in under my name.

He had arrears on almost every bill he needed to pay. His electricity and gas were on the verge of being cut off - Martin said his lodgers had run up the bills. He owed a car loan shark £4,000 which I paid off. Bailiffs came to the door frequently, threatening to take our possessions from the house. In all the bankruptcy and debt I'd inherited from David I'd never experienced bailiffs before. They were so intimidating and the situation seemed so degrading that I paid £80 to one just so they'd go away.

"Don't promise to be responsible for someone else's debts. If you should be unable to pay, they will even take away your bed." **Proverbs 22:3:26-27**

Martin blamed his depression and looked pitiful. He told me, in an uncharacteristically honest moment that, "he never wanted to struggle like his father." His family had never had money which had embarrassed him throughout his younger years. Everything they'd owned was old or second-hand which seemed to fuel his need for flash boys' toys and nice cars. His sister was similarly obsessed with her image. It seemed shallow to me but having money, or giving the impression he had money, seemed to be important to Martin Unfortunately, he'd run up lots of debts to this aim.

"If you have to choose between a good reputation and great wealth, choose a good reputation." **Proverbs 22:22**

Mentally, I rolled my sleeves up and thought, "We'll sort it. Love is unconditional". I arranged for my name to go on Martin's mortgage so I could deal with the arrears, as he was critically behind with his payments. Within months I had this sorted out. I also wrote letters to every debtor asking for an agreement that he could afford. I explained his mental state and how things had got on top of him, out of hand; the companies either wiped his debt clean or asked for a vastly reduced amount. I paid these arrears for him and also gave him my phone.

I wanted the situation dealt with as I was terrified of going through bankruptcy again. Martin just left me to it. He was still on benefits and received £80 per fortnight but constantly moaned he had no money. He gave me £40 each time towards the bills and food but always made an excuse to where the other half of his benefits went. I eventually started leaving him some money each morning. I didn't know at that point that this other £40 went straight on a line of cocaine. Surely he knew that £40 didn't even scratch the surface of the bills that needed to be paid or how much it cost to keep the three of us just in clothes, food and water - but neither did he care, which showed the extent of his selfishness. But at this point, I was oblivious, just pleased I could help him.

My experience with bankruptcy had given me the skills and knowledge needed to tackle Martin's arrears and debtors. I felt useful and appreciated. I knew his situation wouldn't last forever as I'd been able to get credit again eventually. I was helping to get Martin back on his feet which made me feel that this was my purpose; I was meant to meet him and bring order and help to his life. My faith helped me to believe that he needed me. I felt like a rescuer, like I had with Mum and David, like a fairy swooping down and picking people's mess up. My experience in life had brought me to Martin, because God knew I could help him.

It wasn't long before my business was bursting at the seams. I'd built it well following my own debt crisis and was now a victim of my own success. I needed to expand into bigger premises. I decided to move to a larger salon with a higher square footage in a nearby affluent area. As this was a lot bigger it meant taking on more staff. It wasn't long before it was running well which meant we had more money coming in. Money wasn't the driving force for me in my business - I just saw it that I could help more clients both look good and feel good; if money came as a result of this, it was just a bonus.

Despite the blooming business, the downside meant more stress. I had a larger staff force, higher costs and because the salon was doing so well it meant longer hours and a bigger workload. Steering a larger business meant more commitment and a higher injection of passion to drive it forward. I'd finally arrive home after each hectic day to find the house as I'd left it. Martin still wasn't working and had every opportunity to help me out - even just tidying and hoovering up would have made a difference but he did nothing.

I'd started investing in the house we now had together. I changed his tatty furniture for new stuff; I replaced the kitchen, bathroom and windows and had a conservatory and decking put in. The garden had been a right mess when I'd moved in and I spent hours hacking away at it to get it looking decent, all while Martin lazed about in bed. Family life seemed okay as we had a more 'normal' existence. The house was smart and clean and there was less stress on Martin because I was taking care of his debts and the squalor he'd been wallowing in.

We might have been happier and more like a family unit to the outside world but there was always something that didn't feel quite right - a sort of 'elephant in the room'. I put on a united front whenever people came to the house, though admittedly, even after I'd overhauled the place, my friends and family didn't come near.

One friend of Martin's came round a lot, (I found out much later that he was a drug dealer. Martin carried the drugs round for him and drove him to deals - what's known as a 'ferrier'. He provided Martin with his own supply as payment for chauffeuring him around, though he wasn't the only source. I reported him after Martin and I split up, under their 'dob a dealer' initiative, though the guy was in prison in Spain at that point). Martin would often pop out to see a 'friend'; one time I went with him to Sheffield and was a bit puzzled why we were driving round looking for a certain address. Surely he'd know where his friend lived? We ended up on a council estate and I stayed in the car as Martin knocked on the door of a scruffy-looking house. A woman answered and I saw something being exchanged. Within minutes Martin was back in the car and I questioned him about what I'd seen. Normally I didn't question anything but it seemed obvious to anyone what had just happened. Martin fobbed me off in his usual manner but my suspicions were aroused. I found out later that it had been Viagra he'd bought from the woman in Sheffield.

Once I was formally living with Martin I realised the extent of his obsessive nature, almost like someone suffering from OCD. It certainly wasn't a fear of his surroundings not being clean and in order, judging by the state the house had been in, but the way he carried out his routine. He'd go training to the gym but be gone for four to five hours - that's if he did actually go there. Sometimes, if I rang his phone, he'd say he was on his way home from Wakefield when he was supposed to be in Barnsley.

"There's been a diversion," he'd claim.

I had a feeling he may have been seeing someone else but if I asked him he'd call me paranoid. He could come home in such a temper or a truly foul mood, smashing and banging doors. I'd be back to walking on eggshells, fearful of fuelling his anger further - just like with Mum and David.

"You're making it up. I never said that," he'd swear. Mum used to say that too. Then I'd doubt myself. Perhaps I'd got it all wrong?

"What have I done?" I'd question myself.

He got a lock put on the third bedroom door; at the time I thought he just wanted his own space but now I think he was taking his drugs there - his moods point to a 'coming down' from whatever stimulant or opiate he was taking. He'd lash out at Jordan as well as me, saying my son was getting on his nerves.

One day Martin said he wanted a dog. I thought it would be calming for him and good for Jordan's shyness too. Martin was supposed to be buying it but when we went to pick the dog up he'd forgotten his wallet. He did this quite often. We'd be shopping in the supermarket or in town and he'd just walk away from the till leaving me to pay. I got fed up of paying for everything, but he'd just shout, "you've come to live in my fucking house!". He'd completely forget the thousands I'd poured into it and the money I shelled out every single day on food and household bills. Surely he could see that the money for his clothes and boys' toys didn't just grow on trees?

I couldn't help but draw comparisons to my relationship with David. We'd been together around seven months when it dawned on me that my relationship with Martin would never be balanced. I'd moved out of the house I'd made a home for Jordan and I just to come and be an emotional and physical punch-bag for someone else. I'd uprooted and committed my time, energy and love into a life where the other person 'took, took, took' all the time. I had no true home to call my own; my independence had disappeared.

Insecurities started popping up. I found girls' numbers on Martin's phone which he shrugged off. He'd stopped charming me a long time ago and didn't make an attempt to make me feel special whatsoever. I was no big deal to him - just a good catch who was in a position to help him out with his money troubles. I'd put him back on track now. Did he have any more use for me?

I berated myself for being part of a destructive cycle once again. Hadn't I learned from everything I'd been through in my childhood and through my experience with

David? Hadn't I built my self-esteem and self-respect at all? I felt vulnerable, which in hindsight, was perhaps the worst thing I could feel. It gave Martin the green light to carry on manipulating me. That's the reason why I didn't walk out at that point, despite the knowledge of what he was doing and the position I'd placed myself and my son in. He'd got me exactly where he wanted me. I loved him so much by then and my faith made me still think I could change him. He also made me feel as if he was the only one who would want me or could put up with me. He made me feel worthless to anyone else.

Martin's opinion of women was disgraceful - he thought they were inferior to him. He'd often tell me, "only be with a woman until she's 45 then trade her in."

He wouldn't just use women though. If he thought anyone could help him with what he wanted he'd charm them then dump them the minute they stopped being useful.

I'd thought he was to be trusted by his sympathy and interest in my past with David but now I saw that the way I'd successfully got back on my feet after bankruptcy, how I'd paid my debtors and rebuilt my life and my business, was very attractive to someone in his financial position.

Had I known then what I know now, it would have been less hurtful to leave at this point. I'd have done my duty, taken care of him - he was back on his feet and on an even keel, enough for me to leave him to fend for himself.

"At this point, take charge of your mind and anxieties; cast down imaginations, bringing to captivity every thought; don't argue, resist or reason with your thoughts, wait to be restored." **Corinthians 10:5**

But by that point, I loved him. I craved his love for me. I still dreamt of a happy family unit for Martin, Jordan and I. Although Martin hadn't made much attempt to get on with Jordan, I still hoped that he'd settle down and accept him, love him as his own, even.

About a year into our relationship we planned a trip to Disneyland. It was Christmas time and I was really looking to going away as a family.

We queued in the airport and waited for our flight to be called. Amongst the other passengers were a single woman and her child. Martin was very flirtatious with the woman, despite the fact Jordan and I were stood beside him. She sat near us on the plane, so the journey there saw Martin fawning over her. She even popped up when we were at the resort, everywhere we turned, this woman and her child came out of nowhere.

I thought Martin should be paying attention to Jordan and trying to win his affection but he paid more notice to this woman's boy. He was a very boisterous lad and Martin constantly compared Jordan, asking why he couldn't be more like him. He even called Jordan a "little shit" to his face.

Jordan didn't like the bigger rides and I wasn't going to force him to go on them. Martin seemed disgusted. "Chuck him on them," he shouted then sat with the other woman, ignoring us both.

Later, I mentioned how much time he was spending with this woman to Martin but he just said I was paranoid. I'd paid for this holiday, as per usual. I'd taken us to Cyprus, I paid for everything, in the hope we'd enjoy these things as a family. Even if something was his idea, it was always assumed I'd pay. He took me for granted.

He had no conscience either. This was our holiday too and therefore I thought we should all enjoy it. The situation was stressing me out when I should have been relaxing and brought on a bad migraine.

"Jordan's a sissy. He should man up," Martin goaded.

This upset Jordan, understandably, but his goading also hurt me too. Martin was always insinuating that Jordan was a mummy's boy, even that he was gay. I felt insecure when he acted like this - why would he say things like that if he loved me? I felt too intimidated to stand up to him, so he felt he had free licence to insult us both.

As we were in Disneyland we'd gone into various Disney shops and Jordan, who was still only a young boy, had set his heart on a Tinkerbell doll. He loved it because the wings lit up.

"Fucking gay little bastard," Martin said. He went ballistic. I remember thinking, "What did it matter?"

Jordan was so upset that he ran out of the shop into the crowds. I ran after him, upset at the way Martin was treating him and upset because I hadn't stood up to him. I was piggy in the middle again, wanting to keep the peace and everybody happy, just like with Mum.

Martin had hurt me by flirting with that woman and now he'd hurt my son. "What a bastard," I thought. I was upset with myself too - why couldn't I stand up for my son? I never stood up to anyone.

That night we watched the Christmas procession, it was absolutely beautiful. Jordan wanted to take the Tinkerbell doll and put it under his coat, ashamed and embarrassed because of what Martin had said to him. (It was something he never forgot either - even when Jordan was thirteen Martin would still bring it up, anything to humiliate and embarrass him.)

Despite this treatment, I didn't leave. I'd made my bed, I thought, now I've got to lie in it. My faith still made me believe that I could help Martin, save him from the drugs and all the bad things in his life. I was in love with him and felt I had nowhere to go, so I stayed and put up with things.

Besides, Martin was always saying everything was my fault - enough that I started to believe this too. I constantly questioned myself and beat myself up over the silliest thing. I must have been useless and weak, after all, I couldn't find the words to answer back when Martin started on either me or Jordan. Perhaps I was all the things he said.

That first Christmas together I was surprised how many cards Martin received from men. Martin said they were from his gay fan base stemming from his days as a stripper. He'd performed at gay clubs and stripped for gay magazines. His clothes had been flamboyant until I started buying them for him - even I'd thought he was gay when I first met him. We'd not been going out long when I remember Martin's sister's friend had said, "About time you settled down, we all thought you were gay."
"Nah," he replied, "I like pussy too much."

Even my own brother couldn't understand why I'd got with him, especially when I told him of Martin's stripping past.

"What sort of man gets his cock out in gay mags? Could you imagine me doing that?" he said. I shook my head.

Even a year into our relationship Martin hadn't managed to keep clear of the drugs or his seedy mates, all of which were making him increasingly paranoid. He constantly thought people were out to get him and he nattered about getting security cameras put on the house. I could tell something wasn't normal about his behaviour - even when we were having sex. Martin was really powerful and our lovemaking went on forever. And I'd never seen anyone sweat so much during sex - it poured out of him like rain. He had to keep a towel next to him and constantly paused in the middle of things to wipe the sweat from his body. Later, I found that this was down to his cocaine use which raises the blood pressure significantly. He also used to take Viagra to maintain his erection for longer, of which high blood pressure is a similar side-effect. I also found that he actually had a reputation amongst his exes for sex lasting a long time.

I appealed to the respectable side of Martin. The

seedy life he'd had before me - some elements still spilling into our life now - involved stripping and drug-fuelled orgies. His warped view of women was inherent, as his dad walked all over his mum.

His ego came from his dad too - his father always knew better, could do better or had more, and Martin constantly sought their approval.

To Martin, women were "as thick as pig shit", which, given the way Martin's dad emotionally abused his mum, didn't exactly tax one's brain as to where this attitude stemmed from. He said that single women were 'whores' or objects. He even thought single mums were single by choice.

"You've no idea what they might have been through," I'd say but it made little difference.

Martin felt that his stripping had given him power. He was very image obsessed and saw all his adoring public in-front of him, begging for more, as a boost to his ego. He saw no beauty or delicacy in the world and was very narcissistic. Martin's mum had put both him and his sister on a pedestal from birth and his dad had spent his entire life trying to put them both down. Perhaps there was little wonder he had these two sides to his personality. I was particularly puzzled how much Martin's mum, an absolute devout Catholic, could be so supportive of her son's stripping career - his dad and sister would even travel to watch him when he performed. She had such strong opinions on religion, and even gave me a Catholic bible, despite knowing how much my own faith meant to me.

"This is a proper bible," she said as she handed it to me.

"Why couldn't everyone just love the same?" I thought, "We have the same God - what difference does it make?" Years later, after Martin and I split up, I passed the Bible back to her with a note.

"Thank you, but I think this belongs to you," it

said.

Certainly, in Martin's mum's eyes, her boy could do no wrong. She couldn't let go of her son either, it was almost as if the apron strings had never been cut. She had a key to the house and came over constantly. She made his decisions for him, from decorating to taking his dirty washing home. I resented the lack of privacy - didn't they understand that he was an adult, and that we were in a grown-up relationship? They had no respect that this was our home, where Martin, Jordan and I were a family. I knew that a healthy relationship was a partnership between two people, of equal effort and commitment, and not where one party relied on his mum like a toddler would.

I'd come home from the salon and find she'd moved the furniture around in our home; if I questioned it, she'd say she preferred it that way. If I complained to Martin, he just stuck up for her and because she loved it when we fell out, I learned to bite my tongue.

* * * * *

Time passed and towards the end of our second year together I had a recurring dream. Always the same situation - Martin sat at the bottom of our stairs with a wash basket in his hands, his demeanour furtive, as if he was hiding something. I'd ask what it was he was hiding and tip the basket upside down. A white powder would fall in a cloud, like baby powder.

I've always believed that our dreams are our subconscious' way of solving clues given to us whilst we're awake. Angels have brought me the truth many a time in my life and this dream just wouldn't leave me. I thought the baby powder signalled drugs and I became unsettled; something wasn't right.

I looked for clues, even searching the wash basket but I found nothing there. Then straws that Jordan used for his drinks started disappearing. I found small packets in Martin's wallet that contained white powder - I guessed they were drugs but had no idea which; it was Michelle who said they were probably cocaine. I didn't confront Martin but kept on searching. I came across a plastic tub in a drawer that contained a waxy substance shaped like a small rock. This, apparently, was crack cocaine.

I began to search in the room we used as an office, through a drawer where Martin kept various leads and wires. In this drawer I found a case. I was horrified when I opened it to find a gun inside. My first thought was that it must have been a toy but I noticed metal bullets in the casing too.

I rang Martin straightaway. I felt sick at the thought Jordan may have found it, who may have also thought it a toy. Martin went ballistic.

"What are you going through my things for, you nosy cow?"

"It's my home too," I said. "I didn't think couples had secrets."

Obviously Martin thought differently. He threatened to ring his mum, which he did every time we fell out. Both his parents came up to the house immediately and took the gun away. They said nothing; they just took it with them and hid it at their house instead. I tried to raise my concerns with them as to why Martin would possess such a thing, and especially in a house where a young child lived. They completely ignored me.

I was so angry that Martin thought it alright to have a gun in our house. Martin's mother reserved her anger for me, for snooping, which led me to assume that she thought his behaviour acceptable. There was little wonder he thought it was alright, she never made him take responsibility for any of his actions. What sort of woman was she; what sort of message did her lack of concern give?

I felt like I wasn't worth consulting in the whole situation. That Jordan could have found the gun and the possible consequences of this was something not even considered by everyone else concerned. Surely, I shouldn't have had to force such a serious issue - in any loving, normal relationship, protection of your loved ones should be your utmost priority - it certainly was for me.

Martin later tried to claim the gun was a replica he used on stage as part of his stripping act but I didn't believe him. The seedier and dangerous side of his life was becoming normal to our family unit now. He'd stopped trying to hide his drug use - one night he even thought he was a cat. He scared me so much; he was so drugged up and the sweat pouring from him was unbelievable. This episode frightened me into researching the side effects of what he was taking.

One particular night Martin stood in the doorway at home grinding his teeth. He said he didn't feel well and that his heart was racing. Within seconds he started being violently sick - projectile vomiting, up the walls, all over, before starting to fit.

I sent Jordan out of the way. I was horrified to see Martin so unwell and also in a panic because I didn't know what was happening to him. I actually feared he was dying. Eventually he stopped, vomit absolutely everywhere.

Once he was over his seizure he started crying. He was curled up like a baby, holding his knees. I got hold of the dressing gown he was wearing and demanded the truth. Twice he swore on his mum's life that he wasn't on any drugs.

"Liar!" I said. I was determined he wasn't going anywhere until I finally got some answers.

"Look, I love you. I want to help you," I assured.

I felt it was important to let him know he was in a safe, secure environment. After insisting otherwise a couple more times, he eventually admitted he'd reacted to a dose of cocaine, and that he regularly took the drug.

I cleaned up the sick and put him in the bath. He needed a doctor but I didn't dare ring one, and instead I left him to rest once I put him in the recovery position.

I took the dog for a walk to clear my head. I was devastated to hear him admit to his cocaine usage but I was also relieved.

"If he loves me, he'll help himself," I thought. I was even more determined to help him get off the drugs.

Chapter Six:
A new start?

We talked it over later, once Martin had recovered. He appeared calmer and hugely relieved from offloading the truth, which made two of us. He agreed to go to rehab but swore that he didn't want anyone to know - not even his parents. He wanted to protect them from the truth even though he'd thought it fine to lie to me for years.

I asked who had given him the drugs but he wouldn't say as he "thought he'd get killed". Eventually he told me who it was. I told him he'd never be free of the drugs if he continued to associate with the people who dealt them - he needed to have a clean break for clean living. He seemed to agree and initially stepped up his gym sessions to keep his mind and body occupied whilst his body coped with the physical fallout from withdrawal of the drugs.

A week later I read in the newspaper that a local guy had died in a car chase two days after Martin's seizure. I mentioned it to Martin who casually said it was the dealer who had given him the dose of cocaine that had made him so ill.

As a result of Martin's seizure and vulnerable state I was in my element. I was finally needed in our unbalanced relationship and I felt that things were more equal now that he relied on me for help. I formed a plan to wean him off the drugs and alcohol because his drinking was excessive too - it was just another crutch - so I got a book from Alcoholics Anonymous about his addiction. We bought books and DVDs about his habit, many written by bouncers and ex-convicts telling how they'd overcome their addictions. He found these particularly inspiring as he could relate to their stories.

I also found a rehab centre through church. Martin flatly refused to live-in whilst receiving support because his friends and contacts who didn't know of his drug abuse would have found out his secret. He did, however, agree to go to some sessions held weekly, each Friday night.

The first time he went he got a white disc to carry around as a constant reminder, with the letters 'C.A.' on it; this meant he was a cocaine addict. I didn't know then that he only attended that first session, as each week he left for the centre. God only knows where he went instead.

I felt that things were starting to level out and my faith helped me to believe I could help Martin. Around this time, the Boyzone singer, Shane Lynch, came to our area. Having turned to the Christian faith following his own addiction, Shane gave testimonies and I thought he would be the ideal person and role model to offer inspiration and support to Martin, so I convinced him to come with me. I spoke with Shane about Martin, showing him the disc with C.A. on it. He asked to speak to Martin privately, before saying to me, "I could never be in a relationship with someone who wasn't a practising Christian."

I took this to mean I should stay in my relationship and help show Martin a clean life - that it was my purpose. I felt that Martin was lost and insecure; Shane's words re-awoke my soul. Shane spoke to Martin, giving him a hug before leaving. This seemed to give Martin a real boost and made him a little emotional. Following Shane's talk my faith got even stronger and I felt much better about things - I felt empowered that this shift in our relationship meant we were more equally balanced.

Martin did make the effort to change. I helped him address the issues affecting his whole life. He cut ties with his old contacts and seemed a much nicer person. My religion helped show him how to resist temptation. My worry was that the dark side of his life and personality was very strong, and the hold drugs and his friends had over him could pull him back, should he ever have a weak moment.

For a while, life was calmer and our relationship felt more equal. We could have a proper conversation with no mood swings. Jordan stopped over at Mum's a lot which gave us the space to enjoy being a couple. She didn't seem to like the fact our relationship was working and I remember the following New Years' Eve in particular; Jordan had stopped over at their house because Martin and I went to a nice hotel to celebrate. We had to leave the room after breakfast on New Years' Day so Mum must have got it in her head that we would be home by noon. Although we wouldn't have been much later than this, when noon came I checked my phone through habit and saw loads of missed calls and nasty voicemails.

"Your dad's ripped his finger open, we're at the hospital. Have you forgotten you have a son?" one said.

I felt so guilty and immediately rung the accident and emergency department at Barnsley hospital - assuming they'd have gone there as it was the nearest. When reception told me they'd had no one of Dad's name visit, I phoned another hospital. He'd not been there either.

I started to panic about how badly hurt my dad may have been and also about keeping Mum sweet. I knew she'd think I was taking a liberty by not returning for Jordan at the crack of dawn. She'd think we were using her.

Martin kept telling me to calm down and pushed me up against the wall.

"Look at the state of you. Look what she's doing to you!" he shouted.

I couldn't deal with him. I was just concerned with finding out more about Dad's accident. I raced over to Mum's house, just to see what I could find out. The three of them walked in once I'd got there with Marks and Spencer shopping bags. Dad had a plaster on his hand. I was gobsmacked. Mum had exaggerated the incident just to make me feel guilty. It seemed as if neither Mum nor Martin liked my life being too enjoyable.

Even though he seemed to be giving his all to his recovery and abstinence from his vices, I was terrified that Martin would slip back into his old ways. The responsibility I felt at keeping him from temptation and the clutches of his old life left me exhausted. Why was this down to me? Why was it just my concern that Martin should know a healthier, less destructive way of life? At what point was he going to take some responsibility? The burden and lack of support was exhausting.

I'd never know for sure if he'd come off the drugs completely, I could only trust him. I didn't want to ask because of his temper. He was a loose cannon at the best of times, especially now, as he tried to come to terms with his problems. I knew he had the strength to conquer them, as long as he was away from his old life.

One idea I had was that if Martin was working his self-esteem would be further boosted and he'd be less likely to search solace elsewhere. I also thought that as well as helping him use his energy towards something positive, it could also bring more equality to our joint finances.

I suggested we got a van to sell hair products to other salons. He looked into it seriously, even flying to Germany to trade shows. We needed to borrow money for the van and took an extension on the mortgage. Martin insisted on both our names remaining on the mortgage because of his debts and the CCJs still attributed to him, but this meant a much higher APR and a more expensive monthly repayment to be paid.

I invested a small amount from the salon and Martin traded in the car that I'd paid off for him to set up the company and buy stock. I couldn't have done more for him but he increasingly relied on me to push him and organise everything, despite me having my own business to look after.

He would do odd bits here and there but it was mostly down to me, as well as the salon, Jordan, and the running of our home. Martin wouldn't get out of bed most days and was lazy, so despite this huge push the business never really got going. I'd cover this fact up as I dropped Jordan off at my parents while I went to work.

"What's that lazy bastard doing today?" Mum would ask. She knew he was incapable of doing anything for himself from the state the house was in when Jordan and I had first moved in. I'd say he was busy with the business and she'd change the subject. But we were all pretending. Mum knew he was doing nothing, and I knew she knew! We just went through the motions. She needed to prove her point, and would question Jordan too. Dad and her would even pick Jordan up from school and park up outside the house we used to live in when it was just the two of us.

"Your mum and you were alright when you were here. Lovely little house," she'd say to him. God knows how that played with his head.

Martin enjoyed visiting the salons and flirting with the staff, which seemed the only reason he went to any. He'd talk to the female staff in such a smutty and degrading manner - he really couldn't see how insulting it was. He'd also get them to ring on a Sunday which made me suspicious - but again, he'd tell me I was paranoid.

I remember going to a dinner dance with Martin and his parents around this time. I was seated between Martin's father and Martin; on the other side of Martin sat an attractive woman. He flirted with her all night, despite me being on his other arm and when I complained he just laughed it off, saying I was jealous. He completely ignored me - I even had to call the waiter over myself to order our drinks because Martin's attention was taken up. I felt totally invisible. Even his parents made a comment to Martin, which was very unusual, and which left me even more embarrassed. On the way home I tried to get him to understand how much he'd upset me but he just claimed to have been networking. He'd given her his business card, completely oblivious to the fact that this was how he'd snared me.

We once went to a local leisure complex and went to buy an ice-cream from a female vendor in a van. She happened to be an ex of his but it didn't stop him flirting outrageously with her.

"Do you want nuts and juice?" she teased, while sorting his ice-cream.

Martin grabbed hold of his genitals and said, "I've got two of those, but I'll have plenty of juice." It really didn't matter that I was stood by his side. He thought he was God's gift - he was confident and suave, always tanned. He'd found a website in America - illegal in the UK - that sold a bronzing product you injected directly into your body. As he couldn't have a credit card or bank account because of his debt issues still being quite recent, he had to use mine. He never paid me back so this was yet another thing I ended up funding. He was compulsive about how brown he looked and was never satisfied, despite the number of injections he took.

Around this time, one of Martin's friends had grown suspicious that his girlfriend was having an affair. Martin saw no problem with spying on this poor woman from his van - he even dragged Jordan along on one occasion, though I wasn't aware that's where they were at the time. The girlfriend played with fire; Martin reported back to his friend that she was seeing another bloke. Not long after this, Martin's friend went round and broke the other guy's legs. This was typical of the people Martin associated with.

It wasn't long before Martin decided to sell the van, buying a BMW convertible - despite most of the money used to buy the van in the first place being mine or from the secured loan we'd taken out and which I was now left to pay.

Because the salon was doing so well, I suggested

investing in property for a long-term return. Although I'd put a lot of effort and money into our current home, it had been Martin's at the outset and Jordan and I had 'moved in' - it never truly felt like ours.

As life had evened out and also because I loved Martin deeply, despite his faults - in my mind, I was with him for life and we were as committed as any married couple - I was excited, believing this would prove a whole new start to the both of us. Moving to another village meant Martin would be further away from his deadbeat pals and if we were closer to Jordan's school, it would make things easier for me - the lengthy commute every morning and evening was such a strain. We'd also be in the catchment area for Jordan's high school, not that this was a factor in Martin's mind - he couldn't give a toss if it made life easier in this regard.

Martin thought all this was a great idea, though I had to convince Martin's parents because moving to the area we planned meant we'd be further from his mum's grasp. We went to look at lots of houses that were all beautiful, but his parents picked fault with each one - one even had the wrong colour bricks! His mum dug her heels in, questioning why we even needed to move.

"Hasn't our Martin done well?" they'd say, ignoring the fact that most of his successes and the way our current home looked was down to me.

We found a four-bedroom detached house in a nice village. I loved the area and I thought the house was just stunning. Although Martin placed the equity of his home into buying the property, the vast majority of the money came from me.

I'd paid for built-in wardrobes and fitted office furniture in the old house which meant shelling out to buy these items again for our new place. In Martin's home I'd had blinds and curtains made-to-measure; therefore, from the carpets to the window dressings and everything in-between, I bought tons for our new house. Jordan was twelve now and he knew how much I'd spent on our new home and how little Martin had put in. He went mad at the amount of furniture I bought and the work I did.

Martin played merry hell for a shed in the garden, going on and on about it. I didn't understand what the big deal was; within two hours from enquiring about one, I'd had it delivered and put up in the garden.

A beautiful new house and dipping his toes into the world of work had done wonders for Martin's self-esteem. He started buying clothes - with my money - and stepped up his tanning sessions and gym visits.

He didn't have the BMW long as he'd set his heart on a Porsche. He saw one he liked but needed an extra £3,000 to buy it, which I paid. Then, not long afterwards, he saw yet another Porsche, this time a turbo, in Birmingham, and told me he needed me to go there and sign some owner's paperwork. When I went, the deal had already been done and exchanged - my signature was for the credit agreement. I felt like I'd been lured into some kind of trap, or rather my credit card had.

Desperate to keep him busy and away from drugs I suggested he shadow one of his friends, Tim, who was a project manager in banking and insurance, which he did. His ego started to build as he became more proactive. As he regained his confidence, it became blatantly clear that he no longer had as much use for me. His chauvinistic ways got worse and he seemed to gain more power by manipulating and hurting both Jordan and I. Where he had once charmed me and kept me sweet because I played a role in getting him back on his feet, he no longer needed me. He had a job, his financial worries were gone - his home and demeanour were respectable again. He also knew that because of my faith and nurturing, I was unlikely to leave him. At the same time, like an emotional punch-bag, he also got a kick from having someone run around after him and care for him with no obligation on his part to contribute. This feeling of power set the pattern of our lives for the next few years...

* * * * *

Martin returned to his old way of life - going out with his friends a lot and spending many nights drinking heavily. He thought he was invincible. He'd never really broken away from his old mates; he perhaps thought he'd be strong enough to resist temptation whilst still associating with them, so it was inevitable he fell back into his old routine. The guy he was shadowing as part of his rehabilitation was an alcoholic which may have been the influence that saw Martin, although likely to have remained off drugs at this point, swap his addictive tendency to alcohol. He'd drink like a fish, like it was fizzy pop. The late nights crept in and the pattern emerged once again. If I complained that he should stop in he'd attack me so that I'd scream at him to go, therefore getting his own way in the end. He'd manipulate me so I played right into his hands.

When he came in after a night out it would be the early hours of the morning. He'd make such a racket with the dog barking or by loudly vomiting in the bathroom that it was a wonder I got Jordan up for school or myself off to work each morning. Even when he was in bed my mind would be in overdrive, wondering if he'd been with other women that night. His insistence that I was paranoid only fed my suspicions.

He hated it if I went out, though. He'd either pick an argument with me before I left so that I'd feel guilty and stop in, or he'd force me to have sex before I went so I'd have no desire to even look at another man. He didn't want me, but it didn't mean he wanted anyone else to have me.

One night I left the key in the lock when I went to

bed so that he wouldn't be able to get in. I found him on the patio the next morning - he'd slept there all night. He was laid out, covered in vomit, and all I could think about was how everyone saw this nice, professional, suited and booted guy - no one saw the drunk, cocaine-addled psycho. I felt like taking a photo and sending it to his bosses and work colleagues.

He was like Jekyll and Hyde. I saw the nastiness, the anger, and I was the outlet for his fears and hang-ups. He often passed out from the amount of cocaine and alcohol he'd consume. Even if I questioned him he'd tell lie after lie - he denied so many things even he wasn't sure what reality was any more.

I got him a drink and some paracetamol and he went straight to bed, physically pushing it against the bedroom door so I couldn't come in and spoil his sleep. Not that I'd have had time to pester him - I had Jordan to get to school, I had the salon to clean, my parents needed my care and attention by this time and I had shopping to get.

Martin must have been able to see how he was affecting others but he was selfish. Everything had to be about him. I came back from a Christian festival one night and Martin was out on a bender. At 3am he phoned me - could I pick him up? I sleepily agreed and he said he'd ring me again when he was ready. I waited for his call, quite awake now, and by 5am he'd still not phoned back. I'd been out all day at the festival and had so much ahead of me the following day, so I rung him instead. He just told me to 'fuck off' - I could even hear his mates in the background saying the same. At 9am he came home in a taxi, and I'd had just a few hours sleep.

If I was ever angry at his lack of consideration he'd manipulate me. He'd send texts saying, "Why do you want me to be hurt?" so that I'd feel guilty. I'd forgive him, he'd carry on abusing me......it was never-ending. He'd get into my head by saying, "Would Jesus want this? He forgives sinners." My heart-strings would be pulled and I'd slip back into submissive mode.

I was used to Martin coming home after a bender and trashing everything. Time after time I'd seen him out of his mind, lain in vomit. In fact, the main reason we had laminated floors was because it made clearing up easier. "Why couldn't he just grow up?" I'd wonder.

Whether he was beating me down with anger, vitriol, guilt or suspicion, it meant he never took responsibility for anything he did or said. One way or another I'd either forgive him, borne from my love and faith, or forget what he'd done because it was easier than fight. The feeling I was constantly in the wrong never let up and I justified all he did. I'd go to church and hear that love should never hurt then I'd come home and think it was my fault the relationship wasn't working.

Perhaps Martin's right - I was a nag, I was no good to him, I did bring him down. He only got mad with me because I didn't do things how he wanted me to - I was in the wrong. And when he does awful things he can't help it. He needs my help. No one knows him like I do....

His mum was still coming over for his washing and taking the dog for a walk while we were out. I felt as if she was feeding his ego and selfishness and that she enjoyed being involved so intricately in our lives. She knew more of our business than I did; nothing was sacred. She could be just as controlling and manipulative as Martin.

My parents were getting frail at this point which meant I had that stress as well. I got so fed up from the lack of sleep due to Martin's nocturnal noise that I bought a double-bed for the spare room and a lock for its door. I moved in there to sleep - Martin didn't care one bit. If anything, this gave him the green light to stay out later. He wouldn't even go out until 10pm because he had no reason now to try and be back at an earthly hour. My brother would say, "Where does anyone go at that time?"

Martin would often jump in the shower when he came in. If I asked the next morning why he'd not just get one in the morning, he'd claim he couldn't sleep without getting rid of the smell of smoke.

Though Martin threw it back in my face constantly, I didn't see my swapping bedrooms as a point-scoring move - it was out of necessity just to get some sleep. The lack of it was starting to affect my health. I'd wake up at 5.30am wanting to claw my head off. Banging, pounding migraines were coming more often and I'd be violently sick. The pain was so bad, it made the migraines debilitating. I blacked out twice, collapsing at work - on one of the occasions I went to sit on a stool to cut someone's hair and the pain in my head and distorted vision saw me miss the stool completely. I lost count of the number of times staff would send me home in a taxi and twice ended up in casualty. One of the migraines was so severe the doctor told me it was like a mini-stroke. The cluster of migraine pain had left me shaking, the left side of my body had lost feeling and I was dribbling involuntarily. My GP gave me pethidine for the pain and I ended up strapped to a heart monitor for 24 hours.

I phoned Martin to tell him. He was at the gym and said he couldn't come there as he had to finish his training first - that's how important I was to him. I got sent for MRI scans but he never came. He wasn't interested in the slightest. Many a time I'd ring him to say how ill I felt and I'd be greeted with a "fuck off." He said I was getting the headaches because I was mental - "fucked up" as he put it.

Neither the strain I was under nor the pain I was experiencing at that time stopped him from abusing me. Just before I moved bedrooms, we'd been arguing over something and he'd grabbed the tablets I'd been prescribed for the migraines - he tried shoving them down my throat.

"Take these! I can't be done with you, I need to get

rid." I had to fight him off to stop him.

The stress all this was having on my body brought panic attacks, on top of everything else that I had to contend with. Just hearing Martin shout a harmless question up the stairs saw me shake like a leaf in the bathroom, my heart racing. I was so scared of getting the question wrong. I looked in the mirror and just thought, "It shouldn't be like this." I knew - and as I imagine you'll know, reading this - it wasn't normal. The realisation was one thing, having the strength to do something about it was another.

"God is our shelter and our strength, always ready to help in times of trouble." Psalms 46

Martin liked to keep me broken and never lost a chance to belittle me or smash any shred of confidence I held. Everyone knew how good a businesswoman I was and how successful any salon I'd worked in or owned had been. Even though the success I enjoyed paid his bills, bought his treats and toys and funded the beautiful house he lived in, he'd spit at me, "It's a poxy business! You're thick - you're just a fucking hairdresser!"

There was little wonder I had no confidence. He didn't get that this 'poxy' business had bought him his Porsche and cleared his debts. Working for myself suited him too as I was isolated - I had staff but few could talk to me on anything but a professional level, as you'd expect in any business. Had I worked with colleagues who had time to spend gossiping, I may have got ideas in my head about leaving him and the confidence to believe I was worth more. As it was, my business was just an escape and not a source of strength to tackle his behaviour. At work I was professional - whatever had happened that morning or last night stayed at home. I focused solely on the salon and my customers.

Despite the nastiness he displayed, I still lavished my love on Martin. I'd leave him little love notes or chocolate hearts on the pillow in his bedroom, or place an AA book and newspaper clippings that could help him where he could read them in private. I refused to give up on him. He'd taunt me and say if we split up it would be my fault because I'd moved out of our bedroom. This helped plant the seed that he was already seeing someone else.

Martin landed a job with a large insurance company around this time which meant frequent stays away or trips abroad.

"He tells you he's working away," Mum would taunt.

I didn't want to believe he'd be doing anything else, though when I look back I have little faith he wasn't cheating on me when out of sight.

Martin's obsession with the gym grew even worse as his ego spiralled out of control. He had an addictive personality, which meant that it wasn't just alcohol or substances he'd get high on - if something took his interest it would be all he'd think about.

He switched to a gym in Wakefield, run from what looked like a warehouse. He became friendly with the guy who ran it - he was from Bridlington but he looked like someone from the Mafia. The guy's teeth were all missing and he'd had one of his eyes gouged at some point. I only went once with Martin to the place - it was when he owed some money to this Mafia guy. The gym had this glass cabinet that housed knives and guns, Martin claimed they were just on show. The training he was obsessed with, though, was cage-fighting, and defending yourself with weapons. He once told me he'd had a thing for guns since he was 15; his friend's dad had let him 'play' with one at the time and it had made him feel exhilarated.

Other gym-goers included a guy who'd trained in Israel. Martin became fascinated with these hard-nuts, even preaching to me that "it doesn't hurt when you die" because the 'Israel' guy had told him. God only knows how the man knew this.

One weekend the gym group went to see Alex Reid, a prominent cage-fighter, in action. I was a bit upset by this because Martin had worked away all the previous week and I felt he should want to spend the weekend with me but I was last on the list. Despite his mind games and manipulation, I genuinely missed Martin when he was away. Why didn't he feel the same about me?

His recent behaviour had led me to believe he was back on the drugs. I couldn't shake this feeling that something was going on. The day before the fight I checked his wallet and was devastated to find a small polythene bag with white powder tucked inside. My heart sank but I had my answer. I left things as I'd found them and resolved to say nothing for the moment.

Martin went off to the fight on the Saturday which was always a busy day at the salon. I had a million and one things to do (and pay for) so the injustice wasn't lost on me that he left for a cracking day out with his mates as long hours at work stretched before me. It had been busier than usual that Saturday and after being on my feet all day, with bags of towels to wash and dry before opening up again, I was looking forward to a peaceful house and a nice cuppa.

I walked in to find the house an absolute tip. Martin had got ready for his day out leaving his dirty underwear and clothes on the bathroom floor - he'd even left his toenail clippings in the sink for me to clear up! There wasn't such as a drop of milk in the fridge for me to have that cuppa. Nothing mattered to him as long as he got to go out and do what he wanted. It didn't matter that I'd had a hard day. I can imagine he'd even thought, "Oh, Jayne will clear that up."

Although this wasn't the first time I'd walked in to such a mess left by the selfish sod, it just wound me up more than ever that day. My feet were itching because they ached that much and I was so knackered. I'd had to pick

Jordan up too because Martin never offered to help out - Jordan was "my son" and therefore didn't even warrant his care or attention. Neither, it seems, did I.

I sent him a sarcastic text message about being the maid of the house and his lack of consideration, signing off, "From Cinderella". He'd passed it round his friends, saying, "Look what I have to put up with". I can just imagine their replies, as they were all chauvinists: "I wouldn't put up with that, mate!"

They wouldn't have a clue (nor would they care) what I did in that house - the things I paid for, the running about I did after Martin, the abuse I took. The realisation of what I'd found in Martin's wallet the day before, on top of his 'don't care' attitude about me, the lack of respect towards Jordan and our dysfunctional lives together made me feel sick to my stomach. All that work we'd done to get him away from the drugs scene and quash his addiction, it was all for nothing. I'd believed I could help him, save him from a downward spiral, but his mates had proved too much of an influence. He was a self-centred pig and I was just fighting a losing battle.

I'd failed to get through to him. I could try again but I remembered how hard it had been to get Martin to even admit that he was on drugs the first time round. There's so little understanding or realisation from someone addicted to a substance - they're away with the fairies. They even believe 95 per cent of people also take drugs as it makes them feel their intake is justified. It helps them to play down the seriousness but it just bewilders those trying to help them.

I didn't give up on him there and then, though. I wrote him notes and left them on his pillow, still trying to make him see how much better things would be if he dropped his friends, his habits and his lifestyle, but it was a waste of time. I cried so much I felt hollow - I couldn't help him after all. He was a lost cause.

"Lie down that we may walk over you" and you have laid your body like the ground, and as the street, for those who walk over. God makes a promise to those who feel downtrodden, therefore please hear this, you afflicted... see I have taken out of your hand, the cup of trembling you shall no longer drink, but I will put it into the hands of those who afflict you." **Isaiah 51:21-24**

* * * * *

Martin got very friendly with another guy from the gym who said he was an ex-SAS man. He referred to him only as Brian, and when I asked more about him, Martin said he wasn't allowed to divulge any further details to protect his identity. Brian's wife was Russian and Martin was forever nattering for the four of us to go out - he was obsessed with this guy, he worshipped him. He even got him a job at the insurance company which made them even thicker as friends.

We went out as a foursome one Saturday night and Martin, Brian and Brian's wife, Tatiana, spent the whole night talking about Russia and fighting. Brian had set up a martial arts school and told Martin to look at the company's website. When he later visited the site online there were pictures of men with balaclavas on it and descriptions of army manoeuvres. Martin was particularly interested in discussing torture techniques and SAS methods with Brian; I felt very uncomfortable on that night out. When I said this aloud, all three of them started laughing. Tatiana said this kind of thing was a way of life in Russia.

"It's not my way of life," I said. I felt ganged up on and just wanted to go home.

The excitement in Martin's eyes as they talked about torturing people and his thirst for violence frightened me. He seemed completely in awe of Brian and they discussed keeping victims awake or playing loud music on loop to terrorise and torture them.

Around then, one of my staff at the salon was going through a difficult time after finding her son on drugs. I told Martin about it, who said, "If she wants, I'll take him up on the moors and pour water over him but pretend it's petrol. That'll scare the shit out of him."

He became more and more obnoxious, fanatical about this 'underworld' way of life. Martin talked me into going out with Brian and Tatiana again and arranged for one of his cabbie mates to pick us all up. We got lost when trying to find their house in Huddersfield so Martin wound down the window and asked two girls for directions. He was flirting and smutty with them, again, oblivious to how I felt. I thought, "If he's like that when I am here, what the hell is he like when I'm not?" I felt completely invisible.

Tatiana was on edge when we eventually got in the club. She told me she'd questioned a bag that Brian had brought in with him, wanting to know what was in it. I recognised the suspicion and the insecurities in her as it was how Martin made me feel. If Tatiana said anything to Brian, he'd just say to her, "you're lucky I brought you into this fucking country."

She said Brian had changed since he'd met Martin which echoed my own thoughts. Brian had never been to strip bars until Martin had introduced him to those places. I told her about Martin's stripping, of his seedy past. She got upset, disappearing to the loo, crying her eyes out.

I went to go find Brian. I told him how she felt and what he was doing to her. He bundled her into a taxi and that was the last I ever saw of her.

Seeing Tatiana like that was like holding a mirror to my face. Martin treated me with the same indifference, seeing me only as someone to serve him. I was forced to 'do as I was told' or suffer the consequences. Perhaps one day, I would disappear from the face of the earth, never to be seen again, like Tatiana.

Martin had all the confidence he needed now and he didn't want or need me anymore. In recent weeks he'd turned particularly nasty as his obsession with Brian grew. He'd put me down constantly, telling me over and over again that I was worthless. He had no respect for me and had ground me down to a point where I had neither the energy to leave nor the enthusiasm I'd once had to change him. It had been so damned hard when I left David to build a whole new life from nothing for me and my child that I genuinely didn't know if I was up to doing that all over again. I knew how lonely and difficult that journey could be - it seemed easier and less effort to stay where I was and accept what I was putting up with. I was also attached to my home and my possessions. Look at all I'd put into that property - I couldn't just walk away from it after all my hard work and effort.

I also still loved Martin. I'd pack his bag whenever he went away and would slip a couple of Ferrero Rochers in with his things for him to find, as I knew they were his favourite. I was always thinking of him but I never got so much as a thank you in return.

Martin was earning a good wage by now but he still didn't contribute to anything financially. I paid the bills for the running of the home, for clothes, food, motoring expenses and his 'boy toys'. His money was just for him and he'd go out and treat himself constantly - he felt like some new wheels for his Porsche so went and ordered them without even consulting me. I knew they'd have cost him a packet so I went searching for the receipt. It said they cost £5,000.

But only the next day he found me throwing away some out-of-date coleslaw and he went mad, grabbing me by the back of my neck, saying I was wasting money! I couldn't tell him I'd gone searching for the receipt to his car's new wheels but it seemed so unjust to be chastised over something costing less than a pound when he'd spent five thousand.

I did all the shopping, the housework, everything. All Martin was bothered about was getting tanned and his mates. If I phoned to ask why he'd not cleaned up after himself he'd pass the phone round his mates or to his dad. He painted me out to be unhinged.

When I did catch him in a reasonable mood I'd try to appeal to this better nature for some help with our finances and the running of the house but he'd just pick up the large rug we had in our lounge and chuck it over me to shut me up. He thought this was hilarious.

He craved control. One night, Martin went out with Tim, Brian and some other mates from the company. They'd all had a skinful when a young colleague wanted to go to Spearmint Rhino. Martin, with his huge ego, didn't want to go and spat his opinions out in such an intimidating way that this young man lost bodily control. He was so terrified he wet himself. Martin thrived on the incident, bragging to me what had happened when he got home. I was absolutely disgusted, but this showed how nasty he was. There was little wonder Jordan and I were so frightened of him. He knew how to manipulate people and which buttons to press. He knew how to get under your skin, to get you doubting yourself or the feeling you had to kowtow to him. It was easy for him to get you exactly where he wanted you - it was all mind games and manipulative power.

There was no trust, on either side of our relationship. He had me plagued with insecurities that he was with other women when out or away, feelings that saw me deviously checking his pockets because I was so terrified of just asking him outright. He didn't trust me to go out in case I found someone who showed me what a proper relationship was. We couldn't just talk like normal couples, everything was fuelled by anger or spite; every situation had to be manipulated to his advantage so that it was always my fault. If I wasn't walking on eggshells to keep his temper in check, I was tortured by thoughts of what he was doing and who with - enough to see me act as a spy on my own partner.

The way he spoke to me was so degrading too. He'd phone on his way home to order that the garage be kept clear. He could have just asked me politely to make sure he could drive straight in, but why should he miss a chance to be nasty?

"Get your fucking poxy car out the way of my garage," he'd say.

I'd point out that I'd paid to have the extension and garage put on the house so why was it only for him to use? I'd got the builders to put a little loft area in over the garage, in the eaves, for Jordan and his friends to use, but they were banned from the garage in case they scratched Martin's car. Martin put his boxing equipment up there instead.

I told Martin not to talk to me in such a way - I even phoned the Domestic Violence Helpline. It gave me the courage to phone him and say, "get your poxy car out of my garage!" Martin put the phone down and didn't come home that night. This was a defining moment in our relationship - it showed me that he was a bully, and if I stood up to him, he'd back down.

Around this time I found out that the drug dealer who died in the car chase - the one who supplied Martin with the dodgy dose of cocaine that had caused him to have a seizure - had been the victim of a set-up. The car chase had been rigged to kill the guy but in such a way that it looked like an accident. Martin was behind the whole thing.

"People don't mess with me," Martin said when I asked him about it. He went on to say he'd acquired another gun. This terrified me because I knew by now what Martin was capable of. But I also knew that it wasn't right and that I had to have faith to tackle the drugs and guns Martin had brought into my life. I wasn't going to put up with it, so when I was shopping in Meadowhall the next day I phoned the police and told them about the gun.

"Save me, Lord, from evil men. Keep me safe from violent men." **Psalms 140**

Armed police came the next day and searched the house and garage - even the warehouse gym - but found nothing. He'd managed to dispose of it by then. I was getting stronger, starting to rebel against Martin's control. I had an uncontrollable urge to check one of his phone bills and found a number of a big drug dealer on there who was notorious throughout Sheffield. I confronted Martin who then phoned his mum. He warned, "She's coming to sort you out." When she arrived, she wasn't interested in what he'd been up to, and just bawled at me for going through Martin's mail. I ran, crying, to the bedroom.

His mum shouted, "Get down here!"

I couldn't believe it. He was in the wrong yet I was being bullied? I made my way downstairs. I was so gobsmacked I couldn't find the words for my defence.

"I...I..."

"Aye, aye, Captain," she said. That was her favourite saying - she said it so many times because arguing with her was futile. She never let anyone even start to explain anything. Even considering the years I'd been with him by this point she'd still poke her nose in relentlessly, trying to control our lives. She even bought my Christmas present to Martin's sister on my behalf - a dressing gown - even though I'd already got all my own presents to give friends and relatives. She just went ahead and bought it, without even bothering to ask me, and when I protested Martin stuck up for his mum. It caused a row between Martin and I which his mum absolutely lapped up, as she always did when we fell out.

The act of rebellion - the reporting of Martin to the police about the gun - saw his behaviour towards me worsen. I realised that he would never care for me in the same, loving way I cared for him. He'd never change; it wasn't a matter of how I left him, just when. I was just biding my time but phoning the police showed me I had hidden strength, that there was still a little bit of fight inside me. I'd started to trust my intuition more and threw my trust into God that I'd be okay. I was worth more, and although standing up to Martin was still rare, this was only in the short-term. Keeping the peace whilst I sorted things out for my long-term happiness would allow me to build on this strength, looking forwards and not plagued by the hurt and manipulation of the past. In all likeliness, it would get worse before it got better.

Because Martin was so obsessed with working out at the gym he became regimented and controlling about what he ate. It had to be protein and very lean so if I cooked anything different he'd physically throw it back at me. I'd cook Jordan and I a lovely Sunday roast and he'd be sat with fish and rice. I encouraged his wish to keep healthy but everything he did was to an extreme. Despite training obsessively at the gym, he bought exercise equipment and worked out in the garage as well - a sign, if ever anyone was in doubt, of his addictive personality. On one hand, his commitment and strength was something to be admired. If only they were directed in a positive way towards me - I'd have been the most cherished woman alive.

Instead, he always put me down, calling me a freak and saying I was useless. When you hear this enough you start to believe it and think less of yourself. If it's what he thought, didn't everyone think that of me? The more I believed it, the more of a doormat I became to his behaviour. If it was true that no one else wanted me, I had to work harder at keeping this man happy, surely? After all, I'd grown up making Mum happy, saying 'yes' to her, learning to accept and adapt to every situation and the scorn she threw at me. "Never rock the boat!" I'd muse to myself.

Martin would hide my car keys just to play with my

mind and watch me panic. He was always on the attack and would argue about anything. I was back to treading on eggshells and not fanning the flames of his mood, then I'd resent myself for allowing him to dictate and manipulate me. Whether he was stood in-front of me or not, he could make me feel worthless because if he didn't directly, I did it to myself automatically.

He seemed to get a kick out of goading me then he'd laugh when I reacted. I spent some of my time helping to fund-raise for the local park and he ridiculed my desire to help others. "Fucking do-gooder," he'd spit.
I'd phone him when he was away, at the end of each day, to see how his day had gone and to say I missed him.

"Don't phone me, it's not necessary. Other blokes' wives don't phone them," he snapped.

"But I can't go three days without ringing you," I'd say.

"I can. Don't ring me."

Even if he was away for a week and he took my call when he was due home, he'd cut me off and say, "Get off the phone, Brian's trying to ring me."

It just showed how important I was to him; surely I should have come before anyone else, especially when I hadn't seen or spoken to him all week. I didn't trust Brian whatsoever. Martin thought he'd lost his phone once when they were both away with work, yet I received a call and from Brian on Martin's number whilst it was supposedly missing. Apparently, Martin was paralytic and had no idea Brian was contacting me, yet when I told him on his return he accused me of lying. I thought Brian saw Martin as vulnerable and someone he could easily influence, which Martin thought was rubbish - he thought he was invincible and that no one could ever get one over on him.

Martin would go to one of his firm's regional offices in Norwich frequently, but if I phoned him I'd find him in Sheffield, and vice versa.

"The meeting was called off," he'd say, or spout some other excuse.

There was little wonder I didn't know what to believe. Then the questions would pepper my head.

Why's he in Sheffield - I'm sure he said he was in Norwich. Is he with someone else? Does he treat her better than me? Why isn't my love for him enough? Why can't he love me in the same way? Why am I so hard to love? When will I stop being such a failure?

If I asked any more questions about where he was he'd go mad. It didn't really matter what he said - the thoughts I had were torturing me regardless and were far worse than anything he could have invented. Once he came home late and stank of what I could only describe as 'stale sex' - a fishy, sweaty smell. There's no wonder my mind was all over the place but when I did push for more of an explanation I got a good hiding.

The upside of Martin being away a lot was that Jordan and I at least got some peace throughout the week, though we'd dread the weekend when he came home as it would be back to walking on eggshells again. It was like we were living two separate lives. It got to the point where I'd actually look forward to him going away again. I missed the 'good' side of Martin but it was so rarely seen nowadays that life was just easier to cope with when he wasn't there. I was left with my insecurities and paranoia but at least the shouting, the violence and the scorn on his face were also away for a few days too.

We'd brace ourselves for what mood he'd come home in and if he found Jordan sitting in his favourite chair he'd scream at him to move.

"That's my seat - OUT! I'm the gaffer of this house," he'd shout. *Lest we should forget....*

Most of the time though, Jordan would go upstairs the minute he heard Martin come home.

I had no idea what he got up to when he was away with

work but I'd have an insatiable thirst to know, which saw me furtively search for clues - in his pockets, in his wallet, on his phone. I'd never been a suspicious, paranoid person before meeting Martin but he'd turned me into a wreck. How else was I supposed to find anything out? If I asked him anything he'd either attack me or taunt me further.

Because all domestic tasks came down to me, (unintentionally), I'd often check Martin's suit pockets to get them ready for the cleaners. In most of his suits that he'd wear for the company I'd find suppositories in the pockets. I'd wonder what the hell he needed them for and my mind would race for an explanation. He once said, after attending a party whilst away, that he kissed a fellow male guest and tweaked his nipples. I was aghast but he dismissed it as just a joke. I couldn't even work out my own partner's sexuality - he had more sides to him than a Rubik's cube.

I'd sit and think, "All those other girls see a guy with a fantastic job, material trappings and a charming, flirty personality - they don't see the nasty, cruel side that I see."

One night he came in drunk and started goading me in the hallway about my scar from when my ulcer burst; about how disgusting I was, how he hated having sex with me. I was devastated, my self-worth completely destroyed. He was going to marry someone else, I had a crap salon...

"Look at the state of you," he'd sneer.

He'd got me right where he wanted me - broken, unable to fight back, easy to abuse for his own sick pleasure. He once dangled me out of the bedroom window - I was bent backwards over the frame with my feet off the floor. I could see the patio below me and I was screaming for my life. I looked at Martin's eyes and they were so full of anger and fire that they looked like the Hulk's. I believe he would have pushed me out had the window opened fully enough or the dog hadn't started barking. Whatever stopped him

I'm eternally thankful for - he then slammed the doors and screeched off in his car. I was left shaking, terrorised. I realised at that point that Martin was never going to treat me any better, things would only get worse. They were so bad at that point that I couldn't envisage what would come next - him killing me or getting me done over? I can't tell you how paralysed with fear I was, but my mind was convinced that I had to get out. I just had to find the strength within my body.

It was a wholly different type of abuse than that meted out by David. When David was calm, he'd been fine. David's rages had seen me black and blue but the bruises healed and were forgotten about. Although unforgivable, the abuse was obvious for all to see and society would have taken a dim view on what David did - with Martin it was like a sick, private joke between him, Jordan and I. Unlike the bruises both men left me with, the mental cuts from Martin never healed - I'd only need to feel down through some other reason and his attack would come again and again; I'd remember how useless he'd said I was and how I wasn't worthy of anyone's love. Each flashback was like it was happening for the first time and would feel just as raw.

That's not to say physical violence wasn't dished out by Martin, but he didn't need to feel anger to inflict it on me. He could hit me or rape me simply because he was in the mood and it gave him a sick pleasure to do so.

He once rammed me violently against the sink by the back of my neck just because the dog needed taking out. When I got back from walking him I nervously continued washing up, then felt Martin behind me.

"Come on, we could go to bed," he said. It wasn't worth saying I didn't want to, or rebutting him because he'd just ragged me about only half-an-hour ago. It was all about Martin's desires - what he wanted, he took. He'd raped me countless times, against the door frames, when he came in drunk and started to have sex with me while I was asleep. It wasn't worth saying anything once I woke up, he would have overpowered me easily and I'd have got a drunken slap as a consequence. In his narrow mind, he actually thought he was being attentive.

I was very easily physically scared, another sign that I hadn't healed from my experience with David. Martin played on the fact I wasn't strong enough to put up a fight.

I could tell by now that he was relying on some substance. There was no reasoning with him once he was wired - he would be psychotic. He had a way of twisting my words to always paint me in the wrong. Mum called him a parasite, and thought him far worse than David ever was. I never said as much to her but I completely agreed.

Martin took me for granted. I was little more than a slave or skivvy - someone that didn't even command a shred of respect. The house would be cleaned whenever he made a mess, all the food he saw in the fridge would magically be cooked and presented on a plate then replaced again; the clothes he brought back from work trips away would find their way back into his wardrobe, all clean and ironed.

Where were my needs? When was the relationship ever about me, and what I wanted? What about Jordan's welfare? I was so busy saying 'yes' to his every whim that I forgot I had passions or desires too. The more I allowed myself to be treated like a victim, the more Martin pushed my buttons. By that measure, was the abuse my own fault? Is that all I deserved? I'd never dream of treating anyone even half as bad as I was treated by those around me. To the outside world who didn't know my circumstances, I was successful, confident Jayne - someone capable of running a large salon with crowds of customers and an ever-growing staff-force. I could stand my ground with traders professionally, negotiating the path I wanted, yet in my personal life I was a failure. To all others, I had it all. Behind closed doors, I had nothing and no one - even Jordan had learned how to antagonise and manipulate me to get his own way.

It was like living with a secret. I was freer at work but the minute I stepped over the threshold of our home I was brainwashed. I almost felt like a hostage. But what if everyone knew? It would only make things worse - I was scared about the consequences if I ever confided in someone we knew. Would they shun me? I felt rejected enough. I felt paralysed.

All I'd ever wanted was a happy family. A man who loved and appreciated me, a child who revelled in the affection I showered. It wasn't too much to ask from life, was it? Murderers and child rapists probably didn't ever feel the rejection I felt and those who'd sell their own mother were probably thought better of by their parents for doing so than my mum ever demonstrated to me.

"God, give me the strength to understand this," I'd pray, "Show me the way."

The mental torture was, in fact, so bad that some nights I just stayed in the salon, even sleeping there. Martin's speed at turning from nice to nasty just played with my fragile emotions and I never knew where I stood or what mood of his I'd be walking in to. He could have me in tears within minutes, or fired up and angry - either way he'd either laugh or chuck the rug on top of me. He'd whistle or hum, even turn the telly up if I tried to talk to him, just so he could ignore me. He'd also think it funny to torment me in the car by driving really fast, so that I'd cling to my seat in fright.

It sounds daft to most to say he intimidated me - the person I'd have hoped loved me more than anything. He'd snarl at me like a rabid dog if he was wound up, foam spitting from his mouth. His eyes would glare at me seemingly without the need to blink and he'd block my exit if I tried to escape his bullying. He'd mockingly aim his fingers towards me like a gun and say, "I'll fucking shoot you." Knowing he owned a gun made this threat very convincing indeed.

He'd think nothing of kicking holes in the doors or furniture as they meant nothing to him. He'd not sweated to pay for them, so why would they? By making me feel inferior it gave him more reason to feel powerful.

Martin would lay down 'rules' or insist things were done his way. Days later, these goalposts would change and everything I did would be wrong again. He'd claim I was mentally ill because I'd be so confused. One particular barb he threw constantly played in my mind - that he only took the drugs and drank so much to escape our life together. The thought that I'd driven him to the very things that were destroying our happiness was sometimes too much to bear. But the evidence seemed clear - he hated me. Why else would he treat me in such a way? I started to believe him.

The full effect my relationship with Martin had on Jordan I don't suppose I'll ever know - though some of his adolescent fall outs and attitudes are a definite carbon copy of how Martin would treat me. Jordan believed Martin when he said it was 'wimp-ish' to show his feelings or that women were stupid - no doubt attitudes Martin had learned from his own dad. Jordan ran away twice during my time with Martin; one of the times stemmed from a seemingly innocent breakfast time as I was cooking Martin a bacon sandwich. I can't remember what sparked him off or sent him into a blind fury but the result saw Martin slam me up against the door and the bacon fat spray across the ceiling. I remember Jordan screaming in fear but I felt powerless to stop what was happening - I didn't really know myself, Martin's moods could change that quickly. Jordan just flew out the door. It took ages to find him and once I did he said, "I'm not coming home. I hate Martin." He wasn't very old at the time but he knew his own mind. Even to this day, that episode is so ingrained in his memories that he won't touch bacon.

All Jordan saw was anger. Martin would come home from drinking and because I'd gone to bed so that I could get up for school and the salon and he had to catch the train home, I'd have hell to pay. He'd storm in and smash up the furniture. It's not rocket science to wonder why Jordan was labelled as someone with anger issues at school. I've seen his headmistress numerous times - she said that Jordan blames me for his problems. His frustration at not being strong enough to leave and the fact he couldn't protect me tortures him.

I'd only ever wanted Jordan and Martin to get on. I knew he wouldn't treat him like a son of his own because he wasn't, but to torment him too, when he was so young, is truly despicable. If Jordan wanted to play football and his friends weren't around I'd try and encourage Martin to go play with him while I'd be making the tea. He'd go out, and for a fleeting moment I'd think he'd be making an effort, then minutes later he'd come back in with Jordan following, crying his eyes out.

"You mourngy bastard," he'd yell at Jordan.

Jordan would only be crying because Martin booted the ball directly at him, hard, just to get out of playing with him.

Jordan would do his homework on the computer then come back to find it deleted. If he complained to Martin he'd just get abuse. Martin would hide Jordan's things like he hid mine, finding it funny as he watched us look for the offending item. Then, when Jordan would get upset, Martin would have licence to shout at him. The steroids Martin was taking would make him so aggressive, it would frighten the living daylights out of both of us.

Martin would ride Jordan's bike just so the tyres would flatten or kick his shoes out into the garden if they dared to be in his way.

"Brusson pig," Dad used to say. He swore if he ever caught Martin doing anything to Jordan he'd kill him.

Martin would threaten my life as our relationship deteriorated further. He'd say he'd got hitmen ready to do me in by putting bombs under my car, or that he'd drag me onto the moors and pour petrol over me. I was so frightened and trapped, powerless to do anything. Leaving Martin meant leaving the life I'd built - starting over yet again, leaving a four-bedroom house (that I'd paid for) to go live in a grotty apartment with nothing.

But things were getting so bad between Martin and I that I knew the end was near. My self-esteem was low but I knew I was worth more than this. I went to buy a soft-top Mini Cooper and negotiated the salesman down to a good price - I must be strong to do that, surely? I ran a very successful business - I couldn't be a complete pushover, could I? Work had actually become my saviour. I always left my troubles at the door - it gave me some other focus than the abuse happening at home.

Around this time I saw an advert for a house to rent. There was something about it that attracted me, despite it being a far cry from the lovely detached home I had with Martin. Within days I went to see it; for someone who was so brow-beaten I always did everything for myself. I never expected anyone to come and sort out my troubles for me. When I was in the refuge during my relationship with David, I'd listen to the women in there complaining that they couldn't possibly sort out a new bank account or view new homes. They didn't know where to start to escape their situation. They'd fear change, which I could understand and feared too, but I knew no one would come rescue me - I'd have to find the courage to get out of my situation myself.

Mum and Dad came with me and Jordan whilst Martin was at the gym. Even though Mum, who saw my material worth as one of the only good things about me, thought that a rented apartment was a good move for me and Jordan - because we'd be away from Martin at last.

The apartment looked nice from the outside but inside it was decidedly grotty. It needed a lot of work and nice furnishings to make it comfortable which put me off. I just didn't have the energy to do that all over again. Had it been habitable from the off, things may have been different, but its state gave me no motivation to leave the life I had. It was easier to go back. I was trapped by circumstance.

Luckily, Jordan had his mates and hobbies to keep him occupied. He'd tried to get into a good football team locally and had been called for a second tryout. Dad had taken him there because Martin was at work. When he got in the team, Dad and I were thrilled and I phoned Martin to tell him the good news. That morning I'd asked Martin to leave some money towards the ironing lady's wage - I'd recruited her to ease some of my workload. As it was mostly Martin's clothes she was ironing, I felt justified asking him to pay half towards her cost. He was on a good wage by then - not that I ever saw any of it - so I didn't think £20 would break him. I'd gone back home that afternoon to find the ironing lady waiting and no money from Martin. I was absolutely seething.

When I got through after three attempts, Martin snapped, "What? I'm out with my bosses."

I just wanted to tell him about Jordan and the football tryout - why couldn't he just ask to take the call outside?

I phoned back at 11pm.

"You're intruding on a meeting," he said. A meeting, at 11pm?

I told him Jordan's good news.

"Big deal," he said.

"You didn't leave any money for the ironing," I said.

"Fuck off," he replied, and put the phone down.

There were many 'final straws' at the end of our relationship and this was one of them. Proof, if proof was needed, that Martin didn't give a shit about me or Jordan.

He'd do some terrible things to me; he'd grab me by the hair and pull me around then tell me he would slit my throat. Perhaps one day he'd succeed in 'finishing me off'. This thought scared me more than the fear of leaving him. Even if he didn't physically hammer the nail into my coffin, so to speak, his mental torture and the constant tip-toeing around his moods would put me in an early grave just as easily.

It was relentless - the only peace I had was when he was at work or away. My stomach was permanently in tight knots. Only when I was in my bedroom with the lock firmly on, could I relax, though this was little protection against Martin. His physique from his gym workouts meant he'd not be held back for long if he was so intent on getting to me. At least behind the door the mask I wore that pretended all was well could come off. I could cry over my lost dreams in peace.

There was so much I wanted to say to him. I wanted him to realise what he was doing to me but we couldn't just talk things over like other couples. It would be a confrontation which would end up with him either slamming me into something or his voice screaming in my ear, telling me how useless and ugly I was. I'd feel like screaming too, just to block out his taunts. I would struggle to breathe and would see him coming at me, time and time again. I'd be wailing like an animal in pain yet I'd see a wild excitement in his eyes. He'd enjoy every minute.

So I'd bury my feelings. I was lost, with no one to confide in, and lonelier than I'd ever felt in my life.

"The lord says I will give you back what you have lost." **Joel 12:25**

The things Martin would say hurt more than the

bruises he'd inflict. There was no doubt he was suppressing me - where would it end? With me being six feet under? He'd not even remember the next morning what he'd said or done. I'd still be shaking in fear and he'd be as nice as pie. My nerves would be in shatters and my breath hesitant in my throat as I waited for the next outburst. But it gave him more sick pleasure to leave me a few days until I'd relaxed a little before attacking me again. It was like living with two different people.

No, Martin would never change. It would have to be me.

I plucked up the courage to threaten him, saying I'd take him for half the house. Each act of defiance saw me grow that little bit stronger. I'd had enough of his torture.

"I'll plant cocaine in the house," he said.

"Wouldn't you care if I was in jail or Jordan was put in care?" I asked.

Apparently not, as he reminded me of those hitmen he knew and how easy it would be to place a bomb under my car.

"Look over your shoulder," he said, "I know some horrible people."

* * * * *

In my mind, the decision was made to leave Martin. I was making mental plans but hadn't firmly arranged anything. One night, I came in from the salon, and found the organiser holding all our important documents was out. Noticing that all the papers were out of their normal order, I saw that the mortgage details, my bank card and cheque books were missing.

I rang the police who treated it as theft. I told them all about Martin's drugs and guns which saw them come out to interview me. Two policemen turned up; one was nice and sympathetic to my state of mind, the other guy was smarmy and condescending.

"Not another domestic," the second policeman said, "have you tried ringing him?"

I shook my head.

They took some details and left to go to Martin's mum's house, assuming he was there. I knew once they spoke to Martin he'd be able to manipulate them - especially the fellow chauvinist. They rung a few hours later to say they'd found all the missing documents at Martin's mum's house.

They brought the stuff back but the mortgage documents were still missing.

"I hope this hasn't been about point scoring," the smarmy policeman muttered.

I said nothing and they left. Jordan came down the stairs; he'd obviously heard what the policemen had said.

"Mum, why do you never stand up for yourself?" he asked.

What could I say? I couldn't argue. Jordan had a mother that cowered, who was used to looking at the floor. It was second nature for me to 'put up and shut up'. Martin's actions had affected us both so very much.

On reflection, the more I thought about it, the angrier I got. How dare that policeman say what he'd said? Wasn't he supposed to uphold the law and protect people? Couldn't he see how damaged I was and how manipulative Martin could be?

Of course he couldn't. A couple of days later I wrote a complaint letter to his superiors and both policemen had to go for domestic abuse training as a result. I know this because two lady officers came to the salon to tell me. I was thankful my treatment had been acknowledged, though I doubted that it wouldn't happen again.

Not long after this Martin came home with a video camera he'd bought. I'd recently found out that Dad was suffering from oesophageal cancer which was just ammunition for Martin.

"Your Mum and Dad have got special needs," he taunted. What kind of guy does that? I'd learned that my father was in pain and that he may not be around to see Jordan get married, or see me happy. How could anyone use this to insult the person they're meant to love?

I reacted and it was only at this point he switched the video camera on, pointing the lens at me. I shouted at Martin, trying to defend what he'd said about my parents whilst he laughed. He bent my fingers back out of shot to rile me further. The quick pain and Martin's smug, goading face inches from mine felt like a hot iron through my head and heart. Tears sprung to my eyes of both hurt and rage.

"Just wait until I show people how you go on. They'll see what a nutter you are. You're a bunny-boiler," he sneered.

I was so angry - the news about my dad fuelled my emotions. This was low, even for Martin. How dare he? Why did he have to be cruel about my parents? Couldn't he just leave them in peace?

There was a photo of Martin and I upstairs which seemed to taunt me as I ran from his filming. The picture was a lie. It showed us smiling like any other couple but we weren't. Martin was sick in the head - no one looking at that picture would have known the abuse he dished out behind closed doors. It was as if that photo epitomised what was wrong. No one knew what he was like. No one saw anything other than this charming, charismatic man in his designer labels. No one but me saw how ugly he was on the inside or how badly he was prepared to treat a fellow human being - one he professed to love if it got him what he needed.

I snapped. I grabbed the photo in its frame and smashed it on the floor. Martin carried on laughing, with the video camera capturing every move.

"You want locking up, you do," he jeered.

I wanted to smash the camera up but the realisation came that other people wouldn't see Martin's provocation - just my mad ranting and the smashing of the picture. I couldn't take this game-playing any longer.

"I've got to get out of here," I thought. "He's sending me crazy."

A strange calm came over me. Martin was still laughing to himself with the camera but any previous worries I'd had when contemplating leaving before didn't seem much of an issue. So I'd have no money - it wouldn't be long before I'd be back on my feet. I'd done it before. It would be an upheaval and unsettling for Jordan but this situation must be far more damaging - at least we'd be free.

This plan gave me comfort. I didn't say a word and went for the hoover to clear up the shattered glass. For the first time since we'd met, I didn't give a shit about what Martin thought - I was leaving, whether he cared or not.

I saw an advert for a new two-bedroom apartment with two bathrooms and a garage. It was definitely a nicer prospect than the apartment for rent I'd visited with Mum and Dad. Now that I'd drawn the line with Martin and made the decision to go, I wasn't surprised the apartment offered itself. It was exactly the right time, my angels had delivered my answer and my faith had listened to my needs.

I think I knew before I even viewed it that it was going to be my home. I paid the bond and signed the papers but told the landlord I wasn't sure exactly when it would be that Jordan and I would physically move in.

The reason for this was that Mum had deteriorated and was very ill. She was my main concern at that moment in time - sorting the apartment was just another thing I had to deal with, and the salon was busier than ever. Any loving partner would try and relieve the load but Martin didn't give a toss about anyone but himself or his so-called friends. He had no reason to believe I'd ever leave him and he certainly didn't know about the apartment I'd found.

The constant backwards and forwards to the hospital with Mum was physically exhausting which brought my migraines back. I felt pulled in every direction - everyone wanted a piece of me - when did anyone ever do anything for me?

Despite our history, Mum's illness saw her mellow considerably. She was vulnerable and I think she realised she didn't have long to go. Never in the past had I let the salon down but my first concern was Mum; the salon would have to look after itself for once - nothing would have stopped me from being with her in her final days.

She was sent home from hospital to die. My sister and I cared for her constantly after she came out. She'd been reduced to a baby-like state and needed help washing and feeding. The roles had reversed and my sister and I became the parents, looking after Mum, our child. She only lived for a week from coming home.

Martin wasn't interested, and I wasn't surprised at his reaction. The only thing I despaired at was his lack of compassion - I knew he cared little for others, but even when they were dying?

Chapter Seven:
The very, very, very last straw

That last week was a turning point. I'd spent my life until then looking out for everyone else when really, the only people who should have been first was Jordan and I. Why did I find it so hard to say 'no' to people? The pain Martin had inflicted was something I wouldn't mete out to a dog. How can someone be so cruel and nasty and walk the same earth as me - I would not and could not hurt a fly.

Taking care of my mum in her final days was an honour, despite our history. From birth I'd wanted her to feel close to me, to enjoy the bond we shared, and I think in those last few days her nastiness left her body, leaving a shell of a woman who just wanted to be cared for.

Finally, she let me show my love and responded to my affection with no hint of derision. I was able to hug her, laugh with her - even shout at her if she tried to do something she wasn't capable of (her determination and strong will was still there). She laid her head on my shoulder and we were able to say "I love you," to each other; it's hard to describe how beautiful and pure that last week was. My aunt tried to force her opinion at one point, spoiling for a fight, but I managed to stand up to her - backed up by Mum's love, after all this time. I felt empowered and strong. It was as if everything I'd longed for through childhood and early adult life was packed into those 160 hours. The juxtaposition was so vivid - the devastation that Mum was dying against the calm closeness we enjoyed, and which I wouldn't have missed for the world, still takes my breath away now.

Mum had a driver in her arm to moderate her pain relief from the effect of her emphysema and chronic lung disease. She knew that more medication would end her time on earth more quickly and asked me to beg the doctors to increase the dosage. They refused. She grabbed my hands. "I'm ready to die," she whispered. Although I wasn't going to enforce her wish I felt honoured that she entrusted me with what could have been her final act. Not the twins - me. I knew she'd always thought of me as the most responsible, despite the stalking and control she'd only ever bestowed on me. It gave me the comfort that deep down, she had loved me as much.

In her final hours she urged me to do what I'd always spoke of doing.

"Will you get that blasted book wrote?" she said. Given that you're reading it, you could say she got her final command in - even if it was only realised after she died.

To put Mum's mind at rest, I told her about the apartment.

"I want you to know I'm leaving Martin," I said, "rest in peace."

Mum grabbed my hand. "Never, ever look back," she said.

Jordan was with Dad at football. Mum said she wanted to see the house for the last time. Together with my sister, we helped carry her around every room. Mum wasn't upset - I think she'd come to terms with the fact she was dying.

We laid her back on her bed.

"I'm seeing Dad here," she whispered.

I've read many times that we see our parents before we die, acting as escorts into the next life. Mum looked so serene.

"Mum's here," she whispered.

Despite her frailty, she held her hands up in the air, as if to be collected, before dropping them quietly onto the bed, her family surrounded. Her eyes closed.

It was the perfect passing.

* * * * *

Unless you've lost someone close yourself, it's hard to comprehend the sheer depth of hurt you feel. Although you're numb to everything around you - like you're looking at things underwater, almost - the empty, raw feeling that sits at the bottom of your stomach doesn't ever go away. It lessens with time but one song, one word, one memory brings it back in a wave of revulsion that the person you loved will never share it with you ever again. When a parent dies you feel lonely, even if the other parent is still alive. There's a tangible hole in your existence and you question your own mortality. You evaluate what matters and contemplate huge knee-jerk changes because your life has immeasurably altered forever. Despite everything that had happened with my mum and the mental cruelty it could be argued she'd shown towards me, I'd only ever wanted her to love me as I loved her. In that last week she'd acted and professed to love me that way but the glorious feeling of acceptance in my mother's eyes was gone, as was she.

Martin had hurt me more than I thought I could be hurt, and his abuse had seen me tucked up into a ball, crying like a newborn, but losing my mum was infinitely more painful than any of his vitriol. What most people experience with their mothers - shared understanding, pride, a feeling of being wanted and unconditional love - I'd had for just seven days. Now she was gone forever.

The week following Mum's death was quite business-like, as it often is when you're prepared for a loved one passing. Things like her funeral had to be sorted and I went into professional mode. Martin was working from home all week but gave no help whatsoever and seemed more concerned with getting to the gym.

He asked if he could go to the funeral. I didn't think it appropriate, given what he'd thought of Mum and vice versa, so I refused. Bizarrely, he then asked if his parents could attend. I refused again, I knew Mum wouldn't have wanted them there.

Mum's funeral was on a Thursday, I clearly remember every detail of those few weeks, as my life was transforming from what it had previously been. I was coming to terms with the loss of my mother but also the loss of my relationship as I made plans to move out from the home I shared with Martin.

We held a lovely service for Mum and I read out a eulogy that I'd written, telling the congregation the things - good and bad - that made Mum such a one-off. We held her wake in the afternoon. On the very day I buried her, my brother and other family members brought a van to my home with Martin. Together we emptied the house of mine and Jordan's things. Every item I took had been paid for by me, but I still left most things there. I was just concerned with taking what I could use in the apartment I'd rented - nothing else held any importance to me any more.

Martin was supposed to have been at work but returned as we were loading the van. I was frightened at what his reaction might have been - I thought he'd go mental. I was glad that both my brother and brother-in-law were there.

"What the fuck's going on?" he asked.
"I'm leaving," I said.

He seemed resigned to the fact he couldn't react, given that others were there and that we'd all just buried my mother - perhaps he knew our emotions would have run higher than his had he started. Instead, he phoned his mum, as he always did.

"Mum, she's leaving me," I heard him say.

He went over to my brother. "What's she leaving me for?"

"Do you really have to ask?" he said.

I suppose this summed up our whole relationship. Martin never believed he'd done anything wrong, he was always oblivious to what I might be feeling and he displayed a breathtaking lack of understanding or feeling. I suppose I thought this must have shown my family his true colours but they'd known all along what a parasite he was - it was just me who wouldn't accept it.

Martin got in his car and sped off, tyres screeching.

Most people would have gutted the house but I still couldn't lower myself to his level. I left him the iron, fridge, microwave, toaster - even the kettle - despite the fact I'd have to go buy all these things again for my new place. I even cleaned and hoovered the place before I left and got my brother to set up a telly for him that I'd moved. My sister thought I was mad.

We went to the apartment and unloaded, just putting the beds up for the night. The next day I would need to go buy a kettle and an iron at the very least. It actually took six months of living from our suitcases before I even managed to get any wardrobes.

Initially I'd been glad just to get out but as my anger subsided I resented that I'd been so giving when I left. I'd bought the bloody fridge, microwave and furniture in that house - I should have taken it. I don't know if I was madder at Martin or myself.

He didn't try and find me but he rang constantly. He wasn't begging me to go back; instead, he'd threaten he was sending hitmen after me and that I'd find a bomb under my car one day. He even said he had people watching the salon. This went on for at least two months. In the end I got a solicitor.

I started proceedings for half the value of the house. Martin was really angry at this and swore I wouldn't get anything - even phoning my solicitor and telling them: "you need to go back to university - you're not doing your job right." He seemed so intent on making sure I came away with nothing that I started to panic that he may have been right. I was still on the mortgage, which meant I still had to pay my half of the monthly payment as well as my rent. Even though I should have known I couldn't be jointly liable yet not in a position to jointly benefit, Martin's insistence and the power he had over the way I thought still had me believing his vow.

He calmed down after a while - he even asked me to move back. He must have been watching my movements because flowers were sent to the salon on my day off. This was typical of Martin - sending them when I wasn't there meant everyone got to coo over the huge bunch of blooms, leaving them to think, "Why's Jayne given up this great guy who sends her these? Why would she leave that lovely house?" It was all a show. They rang to tell me they'd arrived, with one girl even saying, "Are you going to get back with him?"

I was so angry, I went and collected the flowers and drove to Martin's house. I still had a set of keys so I let myself in. I'd not seen the dog, which was another reason behind this visit - I'd been surprised how much I'd missed him. I tipped the water that the flowers were stood in over Martin's bed then shredded the blooms. I found another photo of us both which I cut in half and left on his pillow.

I could hear the voices in my head: "And after that lovely gesture…."

This is what he'd driven me to - he knew how everyone would think.

I was so strong now compared to how I'd been when last under this roof. His solicitor had suggested mediation as a way of solving the issue over the house but I'd refused. I couldn't risk him influencing or manipulating my thoughts and plans this way - look at what had happened today.

I never once thought of going back as I stood in our old house. Although I still cried at night with the hurt and loss I knew how strong I had to be. I was stronger away from him but had he walked in when I was there I don't know how I'd have reacted. Thank God he didn't.

There were times after Mum died and following our split that my head didn't feel my own. I was struggling with grief for Mum and the anger and sorrow from the loss of mine and Martin's seven-year relationship.

I'd given everything I had to him but it had all been for nothing - he was a selfish pig. From the outset, I'd been fighting a losing battle for his attention against his mum, his mates, the drugs, the nights out and the alcohol - there was little wonder we'd reached the end. He was a lost cause but I'd loved him.

I cried so much I thought I'd wither away.

* * * * *

Night after night, in the apartment, I continued with the endless questions, crying over and over at the love I'd lost, when I heard the tune of a music box - the kind you keep jewellery in. I didn't own a trinket like this but the music was so strong I actually got out of bed and searched the flat. I couldn't find anything and even asked around the family when I next saw them but no one knew of anything that could make this noise. The tune I heard a few times, always when I was in bed, and I found it comforting. One particular night I opened my Bible and a poem I'd been given once fell out.

"I feel the arms of God around me, as I lay on my bed at night.

Asleep, I feel the angels' touch - I'm surrounded and held tight.

He guards me night and day, always bringing love and hope,

Somehow, I know I will survive, for He will help me cope."

The feeling of being held in someone's hands, protected, warm and safe, was exactly how I felt when I heard the noise.

I helped Dad clear his and Mum's house soon after so that he wouldn't have as much to see to. In doing this, I came across a musical clown and when I wound it up, the music flowing from the ornament was the tune I'd heard. Dad didn't recognise ever buying the clown but I knew it was a sign that God was looking after me, comforting me.

I'd been in my flat around four months when I woke early to find six inches of water covering the floor. My first thought was, "How much more can I take? When will things ever go right for me?" I found the stopcock but it wouldn't turn off. I was frightened about whether Jordan would be electrocuted so I went to turn the electric off too. I'd dropped my phone into the water by accident as I was stressing so much with trying to turn the stopcock off, but this left me unable to use it to reach someone for help. Realising I couldn't stop the flow of water I ran in panic into the street in just my nightie. I saw a light on in a neighbour's house and ran to knock on their door. The guy there must have thought I was a madwoman.

He came over with me to the apartment but couldn't turn the tap off either. He just said, "What do you expect me to do?" I needed to ring the landlord but his number was in my phone. I was still not thinking clearly, I just wanted the water to stop. I phoned two of the numbers I knew by heart - Dad and Martin.

In the meantime, before either of them arrived, I put down our duvets and some new towels I'd bought for the salon on the floor in the hope they would soak up some of the water. Martin and Dad both turned up; Martin took one look at the neighbour stood in my flat in his dressing gown and I knew he thought he lived there with me.

"You've got me out of bed, I was watching a Tyson film," he said. I don't know why he bothered coming because he did nothing but stand there and sneer. Eventually, I managed to get in touch with the landlord and he arranged for the water to be turned off in the road. Martin left with disinterest. I regretted ringing him - the repercussion was that he now knew where we lived and in what state. This was all fodder he could use against me. He had no pity that I was living in this mess with my son whilst he got to swan about in our beautiful, roomy house. This just made me angrier.

The sense of injustice was overpowering. One night after the flood I was driving home from the salon, my mind swirling with every emotion you could name and the list of things I needed to do dancing around in my head. My body was exhausted, my mind was constantly fuzzy and my positive nature seemed to have turned sour. Black thoughts filled my head.

"It would be so easy to just drive into a brick wall. All this would be over. The pain would stop and I'd be free," I thought. I was just sick to death of fighting. Fighting with Mum to be appreciated, to be noticed. Fighting with David to keep our home-life calm for Jordan. Fighting with Martin to win his love. I'd lost on every count.

My hands tightened their grip on the steering wheel. Once I'd had the idea it seemed a good way out, a good way to stop this mental torture, to stop the feelings of uselessness that I wasn't fit to walk the earth as everyone else. The wretchedness was from Martin - he'd planted all the seeds in my mind and now they were flourishing.
"Who would ever want me? What good was I to anyone? No one had ever loved me - I must be un-loveable. Everything I try just hurts me, when all I want is for someone to take care of me," I argued with myself.

Tears stung my eyes. I was prepared. Let this all be gone....

* * * * *

God must have heard my inner arguments and

distress. Before I could swerve from the road into anything, I heard a voice: "Concentrate! Just drive home."

Thoughts of Jordan popped into my head.

"Who would he have if I wasn't here?" I thought. "Why should he suffer too?"

I managed to get back to the apartment, though I don't know how. I was so tired and frustrated - I felt like a zombie. I must have got myself to bed and woke the next morning, confused.

"Am I still here?" I thought. "Did I do it?"

My body didn't feel my own; my mind was still as woolly as ever. I couldn't even tell straightaway if I was alive or dead. Nor could I tell which was worse.

* * * * *

Jordan had his own life and friends to hang around with and now, when I came home exhausted from the salon, I missed having the dog for company. I knew Martin wouldn't be looking after him properly - if at all - and I regretted leaving Teddy behind when I left the home we shared.

I'd agreed to get Teddy when Jordan was younger as I'd thought it would be good company for him, but in truth, Teddy was my four-legged companion. I was the one who had walked him, paid for his food and cared for him, and Teddy was petrified of Martin. He often bore the brunt of Martin's temper when he came in drunk. I'd wanted to rescue Teddy before now but I thought it unfair to bring him with me when I was out all day at the salon. It had broken my heart to leave him with Martin.

Mum had told me not to take Teddy once I'd said I planned to leave Martin but she wasn't here anymore. I'd kept a key for access until the house was sold or until Martin paid me what I was due, so I decided one day to go over when Martin was at work to see Teddy and put my mind at rest that he was being looked after.

I walked into our old house and the smell hit me immediately. Teddy was a well-trained dog and never messed in the house but there was dog mess everywhere. Fresh dog food had been doled out on top of old food in his dish and Teddy trembled as I approached. I noticed that one of his legs was bruised; this made my mind up immediately that I should take him with me, back to the apartment. When Martin came home he phoned me and threatened to kill Teddy. He wasn't bothered about the dog, he was just angry that I'd been over to the house and taken him. He wasn't in control.

Because I had such little money to pay for Teddy's upkeep, through paying half the mortgage, my rent and living expenses for Jordan and I on my income alone, I asked Martin, through my solicitor, for a contribution.

His reaction? "Get him put down."

I sent evidence of Teddy's insurance costs, vet's bills and food receipts to Martin's mum's. I got a letter back to the salon, saying, "We'll walk it." I didn't want them coming near me, I just wanted Martin's help or some money towards Teddy's costs. I never got a penny but at least I knew that Teddy was out of danger - as we all were now.

I heard from one of Martin's neighbours that he'd moved a woman into our old house. I had to find out who she was. I felt a compulsion fuelled by anger that I'd been forced out of our house just so that he could put someone else in. I was angry that I'd not received 50% of the property either, that - at the very least - was rightfully mine. The insecurities and mistrust that Martin had done so well to plant over the years made me automatically believe he'd been seeing this woman whilst still with me.

Only as recently as a few days prior he'd been texting me, saying I was the only woman in his life, the only woman he'd ever loved. I knew he wasn't being truthful, I also knew it was only a matter of time before he'd repeat the same cycle of behaviour with someone else.

He'd neglected the dog, which was bad enough, but he'd also neglected me and my son. He was nothing but a bully who'd managed to strip away everything I had, mentally and spiritually, whilst he endured no comeback whatsoever. If he'd have tortured and abused a child in the same way that he'd abused me he'd have been locked up - just because I was an adult, did that make it alright?

Everyone saw him as this successful guy, so innocent and affluent, rich from the love I poured on him and the money I showered. My money, all those pounds I worked my socks off in the salon for. His car, his house, his clothes - everything he had and who he was - it was largely all down to me.

I wasn't jealous of this new woman but I felt a duty to tell her exactly what Martin was like. What if he hadn't manipulated her yet and was still working on his charm offensive - perhaps I could stop him from ruining her life too? She may have been lured by this false impression he gave out of a successful, caring man when in fact he was a twisted, sick human being. I knew that, if he hadn't already, he would take from her all the things he took from me. This cycle of abuse had to stop.

One night I drove through the village where I used to live with Martin. As I drove past our old house I saw an unfamiliar car parked outside which I assumed to be his new girlfriend's. I phoned a friend in floods of tears.

"Get yourself home, Jayne," she said gently.

"No," I said, "I've got to confront him."

I phoned Martin from outside the house.

"Nice car you've got on the drive," I said.

"You shouldn't be driving through the village," he said, "it's nothing to do with you anymore."

"Don't tell me where I can drive," I shouted.

I'd made a particular effort with how I looked that day - though I was the sort of person who always looked smart, through years of being the consummate professional and Mum's example of making sure nothing looked shabby, whether it was old, new or second-hand. The confidence that I looked good saw me get out of the car and knock on his door. I could hear Martin inside, saying, "It's Jayne."

He opened the door. I expected a stunning woman hanging off his arm as he'd always taunted me that he'd trade me in for a Russian bride. He stood there in his tracksuit bottoms next to his new flame - she stood with long, lank hair, in a pair of old pyjamas. She had her hands on her hips in defiance but I could tell it had rattled her a little that I wasn't this downtrodden, sad, ugly woman he'd no doubt painted me to be.

"If you've come here to tell me about his fucking drugs, I already know," she said, "you've got the issues, not him."

Her voice was terribly common and reminded me of the character from Little Britain, Vicky Pollard. The closer I looked the more I thought she looked of gypsy or Romany descent - she just looked, well, mucky.

I felt so good at that moment. "Oh my God, you chose this scrubber," I sneered.

"We're getting married," he said.

"I've heard all this before," I said, "I bet you're looking at rings as we speak."

"How did you know?" she said.

"Because he says it to everyone he meets!" I spat. "But you'll not get there. Have you moved in?"

"It's nothing to do with you," she said.

"It's my house!"

"It's not your house," Martin insisted.

I stood on that doorstep and told this dirty commoner how he'd treated me, that the Porsche and all his boys' toys were paid for by me. I spoke of how many hours I'd worked to fund his lifestyle and how badly he'd treated Jordan.

She actually looked shocked and stepped away from the door a little. I think this was because Martin had described me as being limpet-like and deranged; to see someone so eloquent, smart and confident must have made her question the things he'd told her.

Once I started relaying all the torment he'd put me through my emotions got the better of me.

"Tell me you don't love me," I demanded.

"You left me," he said, "you didn't want me."

I turned to his girlfriend. "Do you know he was texting me last week, telling me he loved me?"

I had this need to prove he was a liar. Even face to face with both of us he was denying he'd done such a thing.

I showed the woman his texts. Then I left, crying my heart out.

* * * * *

Dad's cancer worsened not long after and he was in and out of the local hospice. Martin must have found out about this and began texting me again. Despite the stress with Dad and our abusive history, Martin had no qualms with using me as a shoulder to cry on about his new relationship. The sheer cheek should have been enough to make me slam the phone down but I couldn't help but listen as he moaned about how controlling she was and how he wanted her out of his life. He felt trapped because she'd taken to checking his messages and mail. I could so easily relate to her state of mind but Martin was oblivious to the fact that it was his actions that made her check up on him. I knew how insecure she must have been feeling and what doubts Martin must have planted, like little seeds in the fertile soil of her mind.

I ran into Martin's mum in the Post Office after this and heard her ask about redirecting mail. She made the excuse that her son was working away and needed to make sure his mail was safe but I smiled inwardly as I knew differently. She had his letters sent to her house, as she had when we'd been together, to stop me 'snooping'. It was all happening again. At that moment, I felt so sorry for that woman - my heart really did go out to her. No doubt she'd fallen for Martin, settling for sparse affection in return for the tolerance she'd need to show for his drug addiction and powerful mind control.

The wrangling over the house came to fruition and I was awarded 40 per cent of the value. I wasn't completely satisfied with the settlement as you'd hardly expect me to be, considering it was far more than this that I'd put into the house, but I was exhausted and finally free of him. It seemed some consolation.

I'd become restless in the apartment so Jordan and I moved again to a house in another area. I liked the property but I wasn't struck about the locality, I didn't feel it was home. I was still angry that my son and I had been the ones that had had to move out of the place we had thought of as 'home'. Jordan felt we'd settled for second best too.

Jordan's birthday came round and Martin posted some money in an envelope for him but stressed that his girlfriend wasn't to know. He seemed to see me as a friend, someone he could offload his feelings to - there was no way he'd have said such intimate things to his mates. His ego and reputation were far too important.

I definitely got the feeling he was in trouble again and that he didn't know how to get out of it, but at the same time, I knew he was not my responsibility any more. He asked me to pray for him which I did. I won't deny that I felt flattered that he was sharing so much with me. There was less bravado about him and he was far more open than he'd ever been when we'd been together. I think things were starting to hit home to Martin just what our relationship could have been and what he'd actually lost.

Dad's condition deteriorated sharply just before Christmas. I was at the hospice on Christmas Eve when Martin phoned. I took the call outside as I didn't want Dad to hear - he was poorly enough without worrying him further that Martin was still in contact with me. I told Martin how ill Dad was and he seemed genuinely concerned. We wished each other a happy Christmas with no hint of bitterness and there was a definite air of acceptance on both sides. We were friends with no animosity; I could help him from a distance and he recognised and appreciated this support.

This closure gave me comfort but my world was rocked two days after Christmas when Dad died.

I rang Martin - he'd seemed so concerned about Dad's condition that I thought it only right he knew. Before Martin could begin to speak the phone was snatched away from him.

"This is Martin's fiancée. We don't want you ringing him again. I suggest you fuck off!"

I was absolutely gobsmacked. I honestly couldn't believe what she was saying. My dad had just died and here she was, abusing me over the phone. Where was Martin? Why didn't he stop her? He knew why I was ringing - why didn't he snatch the phone back and tell *her* to shut up?

I found a message on the answer-phone that also came from this lowlife: "Don't phone Martin just because you're lonely."

She had no idea he'd been phoning me over the last couple of months, nor any clue as to what he'd been saying to me about her. If she only knew how he'd moaned of her controlling and that he longed to be out of the relationship, I'm sure it would have stopped the cocky bitch. I was absolutely livid.

I was also angry because of the timing. I was about to bury my father, for God's sake! I had practical things like the funeral and his house to deal with. Following his coffin into church felt like déjà vu. It hadn't been much more than a year since we'd buried Mum, now Dad too.

The grief I felt at that moment was indescribable. I thought I'd had closure on the whole Martin episode, yet he was the one who'd phoned me - he couldn't leave me to move on and build a life again.

To bring an end to my thoughts, and in a last-ditch attempt to make those who'd hurt me see what effect their actions had had, I decided to write letters to Martin and his girlfriend, and one to Martin's mum and dad. I felt they should know just what had really gone on behind closed doors and what Martin was really like - I knew he wasn't the person they thought he was.

"They'll start admiring your status and your armour, when all the time it was your affliction that drove you to your knees and allowed God to make you the person you've become. Before you can be exceptional you must work to develop a faith that believes God for the impossible, and trusts what He says regardless of the odds."
'Bible in a Year' Acts 27-28, Luke 9:28-36, PS 42:1-5, PR 16:16

To his girlfriend I wrote a list of all the drugs he'd been on, confirmed by details of his first drug rehab session. I included a list of girl's telephone numbers that Martin didn't know I had, plus details of all the things he'd recently said about her and the relationship they had.

The letter I wrote to Martin was blunt, telling him he had to start taking some responsibility for his actions and the pain he caused. I questioned why he was getting engaged after all the things he'd told me about their relationship, and I said I was disgusted with the behaviour he'd allowed his girlfriend to display on the day my dad died. I posted them all at the same time. There, I thought, I've drawn a line under it all.

Two days later, police officers came to the salon. In front of staff and clients they said they'd received a complaint against me of harassment towards Lorna Craven.

"Who's Lorna Craven?" I said.

I was embarrassed and humiliated but remained composed. I took them into the back of the salon.

"You just be insecure," one of the police officers said.

I realised how it must seem to them - a spurned ex, jealous of the relationship Martin had with his new lady. Martin's mum had flown round to comfort Lorna when she'd received her letter. She'd threatened to leave Martin over what I'd written.

I told the police what she'd said to me on the day Dad died, showing them all the abusive texts I'd received from both of them. I explained about the drugs and guns and they corroborated my story from the times I'd called them.

"Say no more," they said, and left.

I found out later that this Lorna had left him. Did I feel pleased, smug, sympathetic, excited? After everything Martin had put me through, I just felt numb. I felt regret at what could have been between the two of us, but I had my freedom.

I was stronger now. Now everyone could leave me alone so that I could finally just concentrate on me and my son.

At least, that was the plan.

"The mourning wasn't avoided or shortened. It was worked through and completed; then ready for the future."
Deuteronomy 34:8

Chapter Eight:
A victim no more; learning how to be a fighter

During the last couple of years with Martin, and all I'd had to contend with, the business seemed an extra burden. Although I enjoyed my work and was proud of what I'd achieved, the emotions and pain Martin left me with meant I felt weak, tired and craved peace. Although I planned on selling up, I did hope to work for the new owners of my salon on a part-time basis, so that I still had an income for Jordan and I to live on.

To this end, and whilst Mum was still alive, I put the business up for sale. Though Martin tried to get his hands on half the salon as we split, he soon lost interest with this as the business sat on the market for a few months before any potential buyers made themselves known. Eventually, I received an offer just before Dad died; the buyer came out of nowhere and was very keen to snap up the salon. My intuition wouldn't allow me to trust this man, not surprisingly, after all Martin had put me through but neither did the buyer help in this regard. He'd 'forget' we'd a meeting planned or he'd ring me well past business closing hours. On top of this, his solicitor only had a phone number and no address. I longed to sell and purge myself of the responsibility of ownership so badly that I allowed the sale to go through - after all, my suspicion didn't prove they were doing anything unlawful.

The sale of the salon reached conclusion, despite a number of demands and processes I thought unethical or unjust. After months of what I consider to be intimidation and harassment, the upshot is that the new owners of my beloved salon filed a lawsuit against me, post-sale. As I write this, I'm still in the middle of legal action to clear my name of their accusations and to prove my innocence.

"God is our shelter and strength, always ready to help in times of trouble." **Psalms 46**

"He will bring full justice to all those who have been wronged." **Isaiah 42:2-3**

I would dearly love to tell you my side of things and I would love to paint my defence point by point, but as the case is ongoing, I'm unable to. After years - practically since birth - of being criticised, browbeaten, manipulated and even terrorised, I no longer intend to put up with it. I fought against Martin's bile, oppression, abuse and anger - the way he treated me was worse than people would treat their most despised enemy, yet I found the strength to say 'Stop!'. I'm not the same woman I was. I am a fighter.

How dare these people treat me like this? What gives them the right to taint my name, to cause untold worry and stress, to try and strip me of everything I've got? Why do they think they can take my self-respect, the assets I've spent years building up again and again, the good name I've earned through my business?

Would I have just lain down and accepted their treatment a few years ago, who knows? God gave me the strength to tackle the most unbearable situations from the people I thought I could trust to love me most in the world - strangers who just happen to have bought my business are no match. I will not stand for this.

"To conclude, let no one give me any more trouble, because the scars I have on my body show that I am the slave of Jesus." **Galatians 6:17**

That's not to say I haven't been affected. The stress I've felt ever since I put my business up for sale has seen me have a breakdown and also saw me attempt to commit suicide for a second time.

I remember the day so vividly. I was stood in my kitchen, staring out of the window. No singular event had seen me stand there, clutching the cocodamol prescribed for my recurring, debilitating migraines - it was more a culmination of everything.

"It would be *so* easy," I thought.

I took five tablets. I had more at my disposal, though for most people this would have been enough to bring some sort of effect. I just felt numb.

I'm ashamed to say that, this time, in contrast to the time I wanted to drive straight into that brick wall, I didn't think of anyone else, only of taking my pain away - forever. I didn't consider Jordan, my sister or brother, my friends, no one. I was sick - so sick - of fighting people. For years I'd asked God why other people couldn't leave me alone, why I was the one who was constantly preyed upon. I didn't consciously project my vulnerability or walk around with a sign around my neck saying 'victim', so what was it about me that gave abusers the green light to tuck in?

All I could think was, "What's the point in staying alive?" because I so desperately didn't want to be.

There didn't seem to be any escape. Martin still consumed most of my thoughts. I would torture myself over and over, thinking, "Did he *ever* love me?"

Whether my long-term use of the cocodamol was the reason nothing physically happened, or whether I came to my senses before I took more tablets, I found myself just feeling sad that this was what my life had come to. I replaced the cap on the tablet bottle and busied myself with some housework.

No one else was aware of my suicidal intentions. It had brought me to the realisation I needed help before I made a successful attempt to end my life. I'd sought counselling on and off throughout my adult life, and also received positive help from my doctor. Although I'd gained perspective, help and strength from the majority of these professionals, their words couldn't take away the horrible jibes Martin had planted. His mocking that I was a failure rang constantly in my head and in one session, the counsellor had to physically hold her hand up to stop the torrent of self-blame and excuses coming from my mouth.

But I wasn't with Martin now. He wasn't there to destroy any progress I made through counselling. I'd also found the strength to walk away from his abuse, surely I could build on this if I found it again within me?

My doctor said I'd isolated myself. He was right; my trust had been worn down, another side-effect of Martin's abuse. I didn't let anyone near me other than my family, I was very guarded. From now on, it was a survival technique - people would have to earn my trust.

Over time I allowed myself to open up in front of those who could help me. All that defending I'd done against Martin's behaviour and ridicule had placed me in permanent 'fight or flight' mode. I was constantly on edge and had to learn to relax. Nothing frightened me any more; in fact, I may have been the one needing to put others at ease as I was so challenging and suspicious of everything and everyone.

The counsellor understood just how cruel I felt Martin had been. She knew that words could be weapons that hurt just as much as any knife and which could never be taken back. She helped me to understand how my own mind worked which helped, because I could never fathom how I was so good at weighing up every client who walked through my salon door, yet so poor at picking good friends, honest acquaintances and loving partners.

As we worked through the feelings I harboured, I could see I'd changed from the person I used to be. Before Martin, I wanted to take care of people - now I no longer wanted that pressure. I learned to trust that people were in control of their own actions and that I could help with, but not solve, their problems in life. Recognising people's behaviour and tapping into their psyche would help me in the future, as would a conscious effort to listen to my intuition instead of ignoring it.

Although I opened up to the counsellor, there was a

part of me that held back. The sale of the salon was teetering and no one, including me, knew what was happening. The counsellor's niece worked for me and although she should have remained impartial during our counselling sessions, she did voice an opinion over her niece's future job security.

As soon as she said it warning bells went off in my head. Here was someone who I was paying to help me with my issues - a professional held by industry ethics - who had overstepped the mark, in my eyes. As usual, they were only out for their own interest. I went home and wrote a letter of complaint, stating that I would never return. After all I'd been through, I found it unforgiveable.

In the past, I may have bent over backwards to see things from the counsellor's point of view but my nature had changed irrevocably. I was a people-pleaser, which stemmed from the years I'd tried to win my mother's approval, but this just turned me into a doormat. This then gave those with the tendency to abuse a licence to hurt me. Recognising that this new shift didn't make me a bad person came from my faith; I just valued myself more. My self-worth had taken such a beating but recognising I was just repeating a cycle of abuse helped me to stop the same happening again.

For Jordan, this realisation is a little late. Years of being called 'wimp' by Martin and his constant criticism meant repercussions in the playground as Jordan struggled with his suppressed anger. He received counselling when he was younger; although he didn't turn out to be a bully himself, the school knew there was something behind his reactions in certain social environments that wasn't the norm. The constant pressure on Jordan when we were living with Martin didn't allow for a release until he was away from the situation, so most of his outbursts were at school.

Martin chose to torment Jordan at mealtimes, to the point where Jordan refused to eat in-front of him. He knew if he left anything, Martin would go mad, so he ate his dinner on a tray in his bedroom. He associated eating with criticism to such an extent that it destroyed his enjoyment of food, and he became very picky about the food he'd eat and the texture of what was on his plate. To this day, he still has issues with food.

Jordan's sleeping patterns were disturbed for many years too, as he was constantly woken by Martin's banging about after a night out drinking. Jordan admitted to me years later that he couldn't just turn over and go back to sleep as he was conditioned to expect a fight whenever Martin got in. His frustration wasn't just about Martin's abuse to him - it also stemmed from his inability to help me. No young man should see his mother being knocked around as the urge is to fight back on her behalf, but he knew it was pointless. Jordan was no beefcake due to his poor eating habits and Martin was still so bulked up and aggressive from his gym visits and steroid abuse that it was no match. Instead, Jordan had to listen and sit back, which must have felt like containing liquid fire as it coursed through his veins.

Martin used to enjoy frightening Jordan, often speeding when they were out in the car just so he could laugh at the petrified look on Jordan's face. One time, Martin drove Jordan round and round a nearby traffic roundabout, spending some of the time on just two wheels. Jordan was sick when he came back in. Martin just thought it was funny.

Another side of Jordan's behaviour was also a gift from Martin. He'd learned the tactics of successful manipulators, inflicting endless guilt trips on me to get his own way. The one saving grace is that he also has a conscience. He's learned how to manipulate me but also the damage such behaviour has. But when he forgets, familiar patterns return.

"Jordan, I didn't say you could go out," I'll

chastise.

"Yes, you did; you must have forgotten. Must be your age," he'd say. Then I'd be back in the past, doubting myself, running our conversation over and over in my head for clues. Perhaps I did say he could go?

The very worst effect of Martin's presence was my recent suspicion that Jordan was dabbling in drugs. I can't tell you how broken-hearted this thought left me. I recognised the furtive behaviour. One day, my cockloft lid was supposedly blown off with the wind, according to Jordan. I went up there with the ladder and noticed the insulation appeared disturbed. I didn't find anything up there but I was suspicious there was something going on.

I was at home one day when a friend of Jordan's let himself in with a key. When I confronted him he said he was bringing the key back to Jordan because it had fallen out of his pocket. I was supposed to have been somewhere but I'd changed my plans at the last minute. I suspected this 'friend' had come to drop some drugs off. He seemed petrified to find me sitting at home when I should have been out.

I even noticed my plastic plant outside was missing leaves, as if it was constantly being pulled from its pot - perhaps for items to be placed underneath. The last straw came when I noticed Jordan to be sweating a lot and his pupils enlarged.

"If I find out who's dealing the stuff to you, I'll break their legs!" I screamed at him.

Within hours I was deluged with texts from Jordan's friends, reading, "Don't tell my mum," or, "We're not doing anything." I even received one telling me what a good lad Jordan was. Something about this last one didn't ring true for me; the language used was too old for a mid-teen. I sent a strong message back saying as much.

Jordan got into such a state on New Years' Eve that I had to sleep by him all night to make sure he didn't choke on his own vomit. The police had brought him home after I'd been chasing round looking for him until all hours. He insisted that he hadn't taken anything that night. Despite my disbelief, I couldn't prove anything.

He said sorry the next day.

"I'm not having this again, Jordan, not after everything I went through with Martin," I warned.

Although his behaviour was mimicking Martin's to an extent, Jordan must have also seen his protective side come into play.

"I won't knock about with those boys again," he said.

Whether he knew I was serious, and that I'd go straight to the source of the drugs as I'd threatened, or whether his recollection of how Martin's addiction wrecked our chance of a normal family life, things appeared to stop after that. I explained to him that there were always consequences to addictions and that all the drugs did was provide a temporary escape - they didn't solve anything, they only made the problem worse.

"At some point," I said, "you have to stop the cycle, face your demons or risk your addictions carrying you to an early grave."

"Put on your armour God gives you, against the devil's tricks." **Ephesians 6:11**

I also described the women I was amongst in the refuges, how they ended up addicted to drink and drugs and how most were involved in prostitution to fund their habit.

"Imagine self-loathing stemming from your addiction, the downward spiral your life takes and the destruction it causes. Mothers lose care of their kids which just fuels the next drug spree. Then, as they come down from the drug's obliteration, the disgust starts again."

It was true; I'd seen it time after time. The men abused women are involved with control their lives and their finances. If women stay in this cycle, they're easier to control. They have no money and no clue where to start a new life, so it's 'better the devil you know' and they go back to their abusive relationships. Even when they do get to break the cycle, they're like orphans - their whole world has disappeared. Nothing's familiar and that's frightening. The strength needed to take this step is huge. And the ramifications of your experience never, ever leave you.

The abuse from both David and Martin even now still sees me automatically get into a car without stepping on the sill, because if I'd have got their cars dirty in any way there would have been hell to pay. Despite being out of their lives for years, certain habits are still with me. Back then, I was like a Stepford Wife, brainwashed, habits ingrained into my psyche. When you've been controlled for so long, it's hard to switch this regimented mindset.

Being controlled is not something that's exclusive to women, either. When my mum died, my dad seemed lost. His life had been so systematic and regulated that once he had to use his own free will and exercise choice he became child-like. Mum had always decided everything - even what he was going to eat. I remember the afternoon of the flood in my apartment; because I'd called Dad in a panic from the water rising at my feet, he'd come from his house in equal fluster. Consequently, he later realised he'd lost his house keys. My father, a grown man, went into a blind panic, as if he'd done something wrong when clearly it was accidental. His manner was pure fear and he didn't dare go home, like a kid scared of being told off by his parents. He was absolutely petrified. Had Mum been alive there would have been hell to pay, the fact she was dead didn't mean his fear or reactions dulled.

Once Mum died it was easier for us all to see just how much Dad's personality had retracted. He was a shadow of his former self, subdued and hesitant. We'd remembered Dad as being a friendly, funny man, though he was markedly reserved around Mum. He'd suppressed his true self for so long he'd forgotten what he liked to do, what he wanted to watch or where he wanted to go.

Given time, my sister and I believe he would have come out of his shell - returned slowly to the man we used to know. But it wasn't to be, though there was the odd sign of 'rebellion' once Mum died. He'd never liked the rug Mum had in the lounge so he took himself off one day to buy a new one. He was so chuffed when he came back, excitedly showing everyone what he'd bought - so proud of the fact he'd chosen and bought it off his own back.

He was largely brainwashed, though, until the day he died. His routine never altered; every day he polished those windows and everything had to be done in a certain way - how Mum would have done it. He was as conditioned as Pavlov's dogs.

Small chinks of revolution came and went. Towards the end of Mum's life she was confined to a wheelchair and Dad would push her into the odd kerb so that she'd shunt forwards and almost fall out.

"You fucking pillock!" she'd scream at him, but he'd just pretend he couldn't hear her or that his hearing aid was on the blink. It used to be so funny, but now it's poignant - it was Dad's only sign of frustration.

Prolonged control - a huge part of domestic abuse - chips away at your identity. You forget what you like doing, remembering only what you were told you liked. You'll catch yourself watching something funny and wondering if you're allowed to laugh. You struggle to make decisions after years and years of just being told what to do. Independent thought seems alien.

I believe both David and Martin were victims just as much as I was - victims of their mindset. They were conditioned to act a certain way through their own cycle of abuse and behaviour picked up from their upbringing, and are probably still the same now. I'm the lucky one, having the strength to change how I think and react. I can choose to remain locked in 'victim' mode or use my experience for the greater good.

I can stand up for myself and no longer am I worried about being judged by anyone. I can't save the world by trying to take on people's problems; I now know that people have to change their own mindset and recognise the root of their issues to ever hope to conquer them. I choose not to be around negative people in case their narrowed outlook affects me. Self-pity is so destructive, blame so negative. Until I accept and work through the closure process and grief from all that happened, I'm no further forward than when I was with either David or Martin.

You may think it odd, but I don't regret my experience with the men in my life, or the relationship I had with my mother. I've accepted what happened and believe God's will that we all have lessons to learn and that I have a duty to help others in the same situation. If I've not been through it myself, how can I ever hope to help other victims of domestic violence and abuse?

"Speak up for people who cannot speak for themselves; protect the rights of all who are helpless. Speak for them and be a righteous judge. Protect the rights of the poor and the needy." **Proverbs 31:8-9**

That doesn't mean I can forget what happened, despite my forgiveness. Even though I'm no longer with Martin, I still have to battle against his voice in my head. In a relatively short space of time, my parents died, I lost my house and my relationship, was stripped of my finances and all I possessed, yet his face, laughing at me, is the image in my head. He enjoyed seeing me vulnerable and distraught. The only way I can beat his abuse is to rise above it.

But to work through the abuse, I have to face it. After we split, I had question after question that, realistically, would never be answered. Why did Martin never acknowledge the hurt he caused me? Did he ever love me? If he did, why did he not try and stop his behaviour? And if he didn't, why did he stay with me so long if he felt nothing - why couldn't he have set me free?

All I wanted was his love and care. I'm still angry. I'm still hurt - it's just that I'm trying my level best to recognise, address and dissipate these emotions. My firm belief when we split was that everything in our seven-year relationship was my fault, and that's a lot of blame to shift. My self-worth was rock-bottom and I know I have to build it back up, one shred of dignity at a time. The feeling of injustice that I didn't deserve any of the abuse is also something I've to meet head on. His actions can't be justified.

Day after day, my head feels like a race-track, thoughts rushing round and round in my head. His mocking voice and vile words spin through my consciousness into the forefront of my mind in the quieter moments. There's no let up but to get rid of them altogether.

I can't stop myself wondering if he thinks about me at all. If he's ever sorry for what he did, for the damage he's inflicted? Does he even realise how low I became, or is he so closeted in his cycle of destruction that it doesn't even register? If only he could walk a day in my shoes.

His lack of fight for our relationship was indicative of where his energy was spent. His fight was against me, not against the world to keep us together. He should have fought to save any shred of good from our relationship. I did. I never stopped working at things between us. I went down every avenue I could think of. Martin never saw me, heard me, or acknowledged my efforts. I was of no importance. The courage to stand up to him was infinitely harder than the strength he needed to belittle and ridicule me. He may have had muscles upon muscles and he may have thought he was making me weak, but I was strong enough to get out and change my life whereas his experiences still have a hold over him. Who's the victim now?

I'd often play out conversations with Martin in my

head and say the things I never got to say. There was so much I needed addressing:

Surely a strong person wouldn't have stood for your behaviour from the off? But I think now that I was stronger to have stayed. Had I been weaker I'd have walked at the start of the abuse but my strength of belief that I could help you with your troubles was very strong, and what ultimately saw me take the brunt of your vile anger. Only once I realised that I was contributing to both our demises and not helping things did I use my strength to escape. You'll never care about anyone that strongly other than yourself. Physical strength you may have, but emotionally, you're like wet tissue.

Would I want you to suffer like I did? That's something I'm still working through. Any sane person would expect me to will a modicum of the damage you dished out to me but that won't change my mindset. You are suffering, every day, because you'll never know true love, a balanced relationship, someone loving you genuinely for what you are. It was offered to you, but you blew it.

Eventually, I'll feel peace. I'll have broken the conditioning instilled in me from birth and I'll be able to use my suffering to help those who can embrace it. You haven't destroyed my faith. I still believe my dreams will come true and a happy family life will ensue, whether it's just Jordan and I or if I meet a partner who can give me what I so richly deserve. My self-esteem is not in the ground but in the clouds. I'm worth so much more.

I don't want to escape or tiptoe around my battered emotions, I need to go through them. Time is irrelevant, and this is why I didn't learn my lesson from the end of my relationship with David to falling into the same trap with Martin. I'd been on my own for seven years, after all, but I hadn't addressed the imbalance of David and I as a couple, nor the deep wounds he'd inflicted. Time had passed but I'd not made any changes. No wonder it happened again.

I don't sleep well. When the house is quiet and I'm alone with my thoughts I remember things I thought I'd forgotten. Martin's words come back to me in the dark, more vivid and cutting than when they were first spoken. The silence in the house makes them seem louder, gathering pace with my self-doubt until they're screaming around my head. Then I get so restless the tears flow down my face. The Bible says crying is cleansing but I seem to cry so much that I wonder where the tears come from. I have to keep my faith that the cleansing is part of the healing process.

"You know how troubled I am. You have kept a record of my tears; aren't they listed in a book and kept in a bottle?" **Psalms 56:8**

I know I'm strong to be able to face the day. My negative thoughts can be so strong it seems easier to go back to bed and shut out the world, but I don't. In my head I hear God saying, "Get up, my child. Put that armour back on. You're a precious child of mine and you're worth more. Get up, get up!"

Even after Martin and I split, he'd sometimes text that he loved me and that he always would. Then I'd get such a feeling of loss that the tears would start again and a lump form in my throat. The strength to believe we're better apart and to resist the temptation to beg to go back remains but my feelings would go up and down, looking to the past then to the future. For a long time, I didn't know if I was coming or going.

Sometimes I cry just to talk to him. I curl up my knees into my stomach and ache to see him again. I feel lost and thoughts that he's moved on with someone else start to eat me away inside. I park the toxic words he continually spat at me for that moment and remember only the nice words he spoke. But the moment doesn't last and I'm back to remembering how he could manipulate any situation. How could I ever be sure that the words of love he spoke, though rare, were not part of his mind games?

Trying to work out his behaviour drained me; it's easier to concentrate on blanking them out altogether.

It's hard to open up to friends or family about what happened, so I don't. As soon as you mention the word 'abuse' people automatically think of violence. Unless they've been in my position they can't possibly understand that emotional abuse is just as damaging, if not more so, than physical abuse. If you're hit, you get bruised. Sometimes you find yourself on a hospital bed. You're clearly labelled as someone who deserves sympathy.

But how can you explain about emotional abuse? The physical symptoms of prolonged attacks can still see you in hospital but there's nothing to look at, no damage for the rest of the world to see. But on the inside, those horrible words, like, "you're a freak; you're ugly, stupid, worthless, crazy; how could anyone love you?" play over and over, like a broken record in your head. Nothing drowns out their sound and the moment you listen, you begin to believe and scenarios start to play out.

"I am ugly; I am worthless, stupid and crazy. How could anyone love me?"

You take the blame for the argument in which the words were hurled.

"Why shouldn't he be nasty to me? I'm not worth speaking about. It was my fault he hurt me - I provoked him. I'm so nasty. Why can't I be nicer to him, perhaps he'd love me more then?"

You forgive him, eager to prove you're worthy of his love. He feels no shame or need to address his behaviour, he just sees a pliant, weak person in front of him, someone who won't get angry or fight back if he does it all again...

Eventually, you're so desperate to see his 'good' side that you lavish your love and material worth on him. You make excuses for his behaviour instead of seeing that he's in control of all he does and could just as easily stop it happening. As the attacks become more frequent and nastier, you learn not to trigger them. Your day is spent either blocking out what has happened or trying your damndest to not set off a repeat performance. You never fully relax; your stomach remains knotted, your appetite disappears and you constantly question everything you do. Your nervous energy reads things into situations or conversations that aren't there, making you hunt the house for clues because you daren't bring up the subject of your suspicion in case you get battered or goaded into retaliation.

To retaliate is to 'ask for it'. You fail to recognise, until it's too late, that you've been manipulated into yet another fight. However angry you are just seems to feed the perpetrator, giving them licence to come back harder. And because you're dazed that it's happened again you believe that the fight was your fault. You threw the first stone, you instigated it. The initial dig that caused you to react is forgotten.

You get used to looking at the floor, so desperate that your gaze doesn't get misconstrued. Your physical stature seems to diminish as you subconsciously try to make yourself invisible. If you can't be seen, you can't be attacked. Even if you were abused, who'd believe you? Who'd take notice of the woman who daren't speak, compared with the silver-tongued charmer at the door with a catalogue of convincing excuses?

Then, just as you think you can't take any more, he softens and shows his nice side. He showers you with compliments that are now left to eternally battle against the insults (guess which wins). Your hope soars that the last time was the last time. You believe him when he says he didn't mean it. You forget all the pain and start to plan your future, now the 'hiccup' has passed. You start to come out of your shell and respond to his kindness - it reminds you of the guy you fell in love with. You realise you're bound together, like two lost souls; no one understands him like you do. You sympathise with him and explain away his nastiness. Poor Martin. It's his mum's and dad's fault. He can't help how he was brought up. The blame shifts.

Then he gets fed up with being nice. Nice doesn't thrill him or give him his kicks. You've been walking about far too happily for his liking. So he starts to wear you down with the odd comment - he doesn't come back with a full-on fight straightaway. You hear the comment and you start to doubt whether your newly strengthened belief in your dreams is as strong as you thought.

"No, it's me, I'm imagining things," you reassure yourself.

But the doubt pricks at your bubble and your internal 'nervous dial' gets turned back on full. You start to feel paranoid and search for meaning into everything that's said, because you need to know whether it's all a façade after all. You're so concerned with this, you don't realise you're primed for another attack. You've become plagued with self-doubt so when he comes at you again, you've no chance to arm yourself. Afterwards, you're filled with self-disgust that you've let another attack happen.

"Why was I off guard? What did I do to set him off, and how can I make sure I don't do it again?

Before long, you've forgotten what normal life feels like, as this ebbing and flowing consumes you. Family members marry, grow older and start their own families and you wonder how so much time has managed to pass you by. You're so used to loathing yourself that you look at their set-up and assume such happiness is not your destiny, which helps you to settle with what you have.

It's a cycle - a destructive cycle of love, hate, hope and blame. No pain killer takes away the vitriol. No amount of pleading will get the perpetrator to take responsibility for his actions. And no one will help you.

It's dysfunctional, but it's all you know.

"Though you think you are bad, the lord sees you,

his creation, as good."
Genesis 1:31
"Though you feel rejected, the lord has cared for you as his child."
Ezekie 16:1-8

Chapter Nine:
We all have choices

Now you've read my story, you'll hopefully understand that it's not as easy to leave a relationship the moment emotional torment and violent abuse raises their ugly heads. Perpetrators are skilled at grooming and priming you for their first attack, even seeking you out for qualities such as vulnerability, low self-esteem and people-pleasing tendencies in the first place. If the same grooming was directed towards a child we'd all be up in arms, but because we're perceived as grown adults who can make their own minds up, it's not newsworthy or serious enough to warrant the same outrage.

Abuse is abuse.

So when you hear of a friend who's been knocked about by her husband, or of a man overstep verbal boundaries with his partner that you wouldn't stand for in your own relationship, don't just think, "Why doesn't she leave him?" Hopefully, you'll know why. What you see won't be the first time, or the full story.

"I have set my face like a flint" Isaiah 50:7

"When we look to anyone other than God to meet all our needs, we're setting ourselves up to be disappointed. Relationships work best when you establish boundaries and a budget up front. Ask, 'Where does this person belong in my life? How much am I prepared to invest in them?' Life's too short to be spent straightening out misunderstandings, hurt feelings and damaged egos."

"If you're wise, you'll avoid any relationship that drains you and leaves you asking, 'How did I get into this?' When keeping somebody happy means short-changing the purposes of God in your life and losing your joy, you've overdrawn the budget. When somebody needs too many phone calls, dinners, loans, or other forms of attention, it's

time to draw a line. You've only so much time and energy.
Good stewardship demands that you invest your life where
there's the greatest return. When people who are 'too needy'
demand more than you have the ability or the right to
give, you've got to do one of two things. First, renegotiate.
Bankrupting yourself to make them feel good might sound
noble, but it's not. Bankrupt people end up with everything
from nervous breakdowns to extramarital affairs because
they're overspent. At this point, prayer, a good counsellor,
and tough love may be what's needed. Second, sometimes
you have to walk away!" **Word of Today**

Because no one knows what goes on behind closed
doors other than those living there, it's unfair to label or
assume things about relationships or people. Just as those
women incorrectly labelled me as a 'pisshead', at the start
of this book, you're just as likely to plump for the wrong
explanation. Just offer support, a shoulder to cry on, and
practical help if possible; the strength a woman needs to
overcome her abuser is immense. The building up of her
self-esteem and self-worth will help her to stop believing
the cruel taunts and jibes thrown at her when she's at
home. Remember, however, only she can find the strength
to make permanent change. Don't just slate her partner or
tell her she needs to 'get out' - her finely-tuned defences will
counteract your well-meaning. Build her up as a person
outside of her relationship - *show her she can be somebody*
of value when on her own.

I don't regret any experience I've lived through. But
God has placed me on this earth to make good use of the
lessons I've learned.

"I can do all things through Christ who strengthens
*me." **Philippians 4:13***

* * * * *

There are many things I'd like to change.

- I want to help other women who are being oppressed:

There are more women than you'd believe in similar relationships to mine with David and Martin. I met only a handful of them in the refuges and support groups I've attended and found the common vein running through them is that they're made to feel by society that they're worthless and as much to blame for their situation as the men they're married to are responsible. Many women are frightened of being judged.

This is wrong. When as many as **one in four women** in the U.K. are affected even in this day and age, more needs to be done. Practical support is already available but no funds are ever present to help women (or men) gain the strength to change their circumstances, to help the oppressed and abused start a new life. Because there is nothing but more hardship, poverty and lack of support on offer following the shelter of a women's refuge, they return to their marriages. And the cycle goes on.

- I want to help young people understand the damage their words and actions can have:

Many perpetrators have been subject to emotional and violent abuse throughout their childhood and are victims of a cycle too. By intervening at this age and helping young men deal with their experiences, it could help prevent them from repeating the negative behaviour in their own relationships. Young women should also be taught to recognise the signs of a perpetrator and receive encouragement to value themselves more highly. Fewer women would be hurt as a result.

- I want to educate professionals as to the emotional state of abuse victims:

Professionals such as doctors and police officers are often involved in abuse cases but my own experience has shown that their understanding of the fragile mental state women can display is woefully inadequate. The strength needed to report your husband or partner is huge. Because blame is often part of the abuse meted out, believing those sent to help you also hold you accountable for the abuse you may suffer does nothing to help the situation and only makes things worse - even enforcing the abuser's condemnation.

- I want to change the law:

Only through the current lawsuit from those who have bought my salon have I unearthed some startling information. Access to Land Registry information, the Electoral Roll and company information is fully accessible to the general public. Therefore, should someone like Martin want to search out a victim who is reasonably solvent due to a successful business, and where they may live, it's not a problem with today's technology. In fact, the information could be with a potential abuser within minutes.

I understand about democracy, freedom of speech and people's liberties to know relative information, but although we safeguard some aspects of our private data - such as our medical records - financial and locative data, I believe, is too readily available.

- I want people to stop judging others

Though this may seem unrealistic, it's the same message God sent us, via his son, Jesus, over 2,000 years ago. God tells us about acceptance and how we should concentrate on loving one another over fighting or labelling our fellow man. We're all too quick to judge people; I was judged as a 'pisshead' on New Years' Eve as I brushed death through my burst ulcer - the physical fallout from a lifetime of walking on eggshells to avoid abuse.

I've suffered from depression and attempted suicide, not surprisingly and though I wouldn't choose to have endured such conditions, I don't believe we should ridicule or judge sufferers. This same energy could be spent helping them. It may no longer be a taboo subject, but we're far from accepting of mental health issues in society, and this is what I'd like to greatly improve.

*****

The cycle of abuse can go back generations. My mum and her siblings were treated abysmally by my grand-dad. Even though they were of the generation where children were 'seen and not heard', his overly tyrannical, disciplinarian style of parenting left his children with low self-esteem. Mum wasn't allowed a view or opinion and no love or affection was given to her - her siblings even questioned if they were fostered. However, whereas my aunts and uncles chose to make sure their own offspring would never feel the same, my mother always harboured resentment. This meant she repeated the same behaviour and saw her feel negatively towards her brother's and sisters' happier lives.

I've lived through child neglect, divorces, bankruptcy, the deaths of my parents and yet I feel privileged to have lived such a life. I believe that, to never experience anything and to be blinkered or sheltered throughout life is just as sad. I know I have the empathy to help other people. I can relate to those oppressed and feel sympathy. I can forgive people's actions and I know how to find peace.

I've found a contentment that I want to share with others. Having the tools to empower other people gives me a purpose, and the dignity I've honed and the spirit I've strengthened, despite everything, helps me walk tall.

I don't blame God for placing me on a path that eventually led to pain. We all have choices: my mum had a choice to bear resentment from her upbringing, contrary to her siblings' behaviour; Martin and David were both victims of abuse before they met me and both had the choice of breaking this cycle or continuing its destruction; Jordan has a choice as to whether he repeats the behaviour he learned from Martin or whether to remember the pain it caused me - I've taken the choice to use my experience positively and not remain a victim.

Awareness will be the main element of all the things I'd like to see change. The power and control abusers dish out is behind closed doors, and they're often seen by everyone outside the family as pillars of the community. Take Martin - he was a respectable insurance representative, dressed in suits and ties all week before coming home and treating his family horrifically. Because their partners are so well-respected, this becomes yet another reason for women not to speak out as they fear no one would believe their husbands capable of such torture. As a responsible society, we need to help women come forward, without malice or judgement, and show that we'll believe their recount. Otherwise, we're guilty of oppression too.

Just as Sarah's Law helps the fight against paedophilia and Claire's Law helps people ascertain whether any new partner has been prosecuted for violent abuse, I want laws put in place to prosecute those found guilty of grooming adults, as well as tighter restrictions on who can access certain financial and personal data. Accessing criminal convictions can prevent abuse; access to financial, location and personal data is not something the general public needs to know of a new partner and actually highlights vulnerable targets for those intent on finding a new victim.

Martin was a narcissist and an adult male eternally dependent on his mother. The fallout from this dysfunctional relationship was a severe lack of culpability and no pressure to accept responsibility for any of his actions. Because he never had to lay claim to his bad behaviour against others - his mother always insisting to him and anyone listening that "It wasn't your fault, it was someone else's" - it was inevitable he'd always believe this. When we were together everything was my fault - he blamed me if things went wrong in his life even if I had no direct involvement whatsoever.

He'd blame me for his mindset and moods, despite the fact only he was in control of both. Because his ego was always inflated by his mother, he found it satisfying to degrade others as this made his sense of self-importance soar further. Having an addictive personality meant he craved the feeling of superiority. Had his mother shown him boundaries, that we are all born equal and how to be accountable for his actions, things would have been so different.

Martin's father oppressed his mother, who, in turn, focused her attention on her son. She had little self-esteem of her own and subconsciously ensured the same would not happen to her children, but this intense focus went full circle and instead, she created carbon copies of their father.

We all talk about self-esteem but finding a healthy balance is no mean feat. Too little self-esteem and you risk being a doormat to others looking to take advantage, too much self-esteem and you show signs of arrogance, degradation and possible bullying.

The effects of a low self-esteem and minimal self-worth are not just harmful to our minds but our physical health too. Depression and anxiety set in as we struggle to find the courage to face the world. Even the smallest tasks become huge hurdles as our confidence and energy deplete. Significant changes in our lives, such as bereavement, moving home or job, divorce or illness, can be extremely stressful but usually the stress eases when the change has occurred and time has passed. When in an abusive relationship there's no let-up. Your stomach is constantly in knots and you're apprehensive every moment you're awake that things will kick off. You can't sleep and often suffer form insomnia because you're wound so tightly you can't relax. Then each day that follows you're running on less energy as you've had no sleep - until you've run out. Eventually, you function on adrenaline alone.

The link between our adrenal glands and depression

has been the subject of many studies. Our ancestors used adrenaline effectively thousands of years ago, as they often had to flee predators. The ability to quickly access extra reserves of strength and energy helped them escape any threat in record time, which meant our race survived extinction.

In the modern world we're not exposed to the same threats of nature. The instinct to 'fight or flight' is stimulated from situations and threats of a different kind, from each other, subconscious threats and fear of violence for one. To sustain the production of adrenaline to deal with the constant fear of abuse in destructive relationships our glands have to work longer than they're genetically designed to. As domestic abuse is prolonged, the glands don't get the chance to repair or renew.

There are many reports that argue depression is a result of a chemical imbalance. Further theories suggest surplus adrenaline does damage to our body, affecting our immune system and our levels of such as serotonin, which plays an important role in depression. There's also a strong link between sufferers of immune system-related diseases and women who have been subjected to an abusive relationship. Because, once the danger has gone and the woman is permanently away from her abuser, she starts to relax; her system goes haywire, from years of overactive adrenal glands, continual stiffening of muscles and a severe lack of proper relaxation. Judgement as to why a woman needs anti-depressants or therapy certainly doesn't help this situation. As a society, we need to be more aware and understanding of the physical and mental after-effects of abusive relationships, without placing labels or compartmentalising/sidelining the sufferer. All any woman will want in this situation is a normal life, buckets of support and some peace. She needs space to come to terms with all that's happened in her life. Until she learns to accept what's happened and works through the legacy of what the abuse has left, there's every danger she could return to the cycle - perhaps not with the same person, but to the same situation.

I've seen strong women succumb to being a victim of abuse. Creed or status mean little, and most women would say it could never happen to them, but the changes are so subtle in most cases, you're trapped, paralysed by fear, before you realise. Even I thought that, and again, after my relationship with David - I vowed that no man would ever treat me like he did. But I hadn't healed or learned how to trust my intuition. My self-worth had been badly damaged and I'd not taken steps to value myself before Martin came on the scene. I thought time had made all the difference but now I realise it's the stages you work through - acceptance, grief, and more - that matter, not how many years pass. Without work on your soul and your wellbeing, nothing changes from one relationship to the next.

Given that one in four women is a victim of domestic abuse, this shouldn't be a topic or issue in the wings - it needs to be something talked about, written about, and something we teach our children. We need to enforce respect for ourselves and for others as our kids grow, just as we'd teach them to say 'please' and 'thank you'.

Bullying is now a subject in school that's tackled quickly before it escalates. Although the bullying tends to be towards the same gender throughout young people's education, the root cause of this action doesn't seem to be met with the same gusto. But where does that lead the perpetrator once they've left school? Untackled? Unaccountable? Undaunted at the prospect of doing it to their partner?

* * * *

Just as we're born with the 'fight or flight' instinct, we're born with all the tools we need to eradicate domestic abuse. There's nothing more we need to buy, invent or apply to the issue than knowledge and awareness. Trusting our intuition and reading body language should be things that we hone, but in our digital world we're too used to having our choices and decisions taken away from us, in the interest of convenience.

Boundaries get scarcer from parent to child as discipline is outlawed. Compared to Victorian times, we've become a world that's many times more selfish and self-absorbed. Our morals are skewed and we're heading into an age that's too fast for our spirit to cope with. The speed of our brains will surpass the speed of our consciousness; *we'll have carried out our actions before we've time to think whether we should or shouldn't do them.*

So, is abuse a subject of nature or nurture? If I look at Jordan, David's son, I see actions and behaviours that mirror his father's, yet he wasn't a part of his life. I blame myself that I wasn't there to balance this inherent influence because I was out providing for the both of us. Single parents have a rough deal, and as both mother and father to their children, they have more work to do to enforce respect and morals than a mother from a traditional family set-up. It's often claimed that children from single families or broken homes are more susceptible to crime or violence, and this may be backed up by statistics, but when you think of the responsibility on the shoulders of a single parent, perhaps we should look to support each one rather than apportion blame - which is yet another destructive label. They're women trying to hold their own and do a man's job as well. We should be admiring their strength and building on that.

Having been resident at many women's refuges, I've seen how jaded and broken the women are in these institutions. Damage has already been done, and although I want to be their voice and stand up for them on their behalf, I truly think the cycle needs to be **broken** completely from childhood, before it spirals, not just **treated** when we're adults. The real opportunities to tackle the subject is within schools - helping young girls to value themselves and to recognise the signs of an abuser, and helping boys who have been subjected to abuse in their home life, to see that they don't have the right, nor should they be inclined, to inflict this on someone else. They're victims too.

I'll go pick Jordan up from friends' or the cinema and I'm amazed at the flesh young girls have on show as they walk round the streets. The peer pressure they're subjected to is so fierce that as soon as one of them devalues themselves, all others follow. They also endure added pressure to give their bodies to boys - most, earlier than they'd like in an ideal world. The television and internet bombard them from an early age with images of sex. Gratifying sensitive, adult issues means that their childhood innocence is short-lived.

Old-fashioned dating and the art of finding out about someone have gone; we can't read body language or interpret the true meaning of an electronic message from behind a screen. Boundaries are forgotten and social skills aren't practised as everything nowadays is instant. Relationships get serious within weeks and the anticipation, excitement and the incremental discovery of someone's true personality don't even factor. How can you know or trust someone implicitly over the internet - they're not even forced to be who they say they are!

Emotions are sparse and your intuition doesn't have the time to make an appearance. Young people find themselves in situations they can't escape from before they realise. The ever-growing compensation and benefit culture doesn't foster a strong sense of morality either; we're swamped with adverts telling us to blame someone else for money. We don't have depth to our conversations and judgements are given out quickly, with no thought to their effect.

Where will it end?

There's no doubt that the internet is a great tool for information and something which helps communities and families keep in touch far easier than before. But recognising that it brings its negatives and a dark side is very important for the next generation to understand, who have it ingrained in their lives. As the older generation, we can judge the level of intrusion the internet plays in our lives but for our children, they have little choice.

It's a sad realisation, but I see a direct correlation of what I perceive as a lack of morals, values and respect with the growing number of women in relationships that feature domestic abuse. I hope to talk in as many schools as I can, to teach all the young men and women that their actions can have devastating consequences. The Bible teaches us more than just religion, it shows us how to value others, how to have respect for our individuality, and how to love ourselves. It's more than a book of faith - it's our toolkit for a happy, balanced life. We *can* still have the internet; we *can* still enjoy all our modern world has to offer, just within the boundaries of morality and decency.

Please help me achieve my goal.

Chapter Ten:
Lessons and references:

"Having hope will give you courage" **Job 11:18**
"Hope is a powerful force. It arouses your mind to explore every possible angle. It enables you to overcome the daunting obstacles. It's absolutely essential to the life God wants you to live. It's the fuel your heart runs on. It's the single biggest difference between those who persevere and those who give up. Hope is what makes couples say, 'I do', without any guarantees, and later, after all the broken promises, pick up the pieces and try again knowing it can get better. It's why composers agonise over a score and artists over a canvas, believing some glimmer of beauty will emerge from the struggle. As an old man, Henri Matisse was crippled with agonising arthritis. When asked why he continued to wrap his swollen fingers around a brush every day he replied, 'The pain goes away; the beauty endures'. Labouring to paint the ceiling of the Sistine Chapel, Michelangelo grew so discouraged that he wanted to quit. But every morning hope pushed him up the ladder to fulfil his magnificent vision. Hope is what made Abraham leave home without knowing where God was taking him. It made Paul challenge the powers of Rome. It's what fuelled the Old Testament prophets to keep taking on City Hall. This is not blind optimism, but faith focused, and hope - in God. 'You have been my hope...my confidence since my youth' (Psalm 71:5). You can survive the loss of many things, but not the loss of hope. Nobody experienced greater loss than Job, yet he wrote, 'Having hope will give you courage'. So keep your hope alive by trusting in God."
Bible in a Year: Remaining Faithful - Ruth 1:3-18, John 6:41-69

Believe in yourself

Judge not yourself through hurt and pain, for you are special and you are sane.

Hold on to your dreams, try not to cry. Live not in despair by questioning why.

Live not in the past, leave it behind. There are so many answers you will never find.

Be true to yourself, you're only one being. If you wear a mask, you're hiding from seeing.

Don't be a pawn in the chess game they play. Use all of your pieces, ignore what they say.

For when they say 'check', it's only bait; with success and happiness you have 'checkmate'.

Let the head rule the heart, the tears then will not flow. When the sun shines it will shine through your shadow.

Your lesson was learned, there's no more denial. There are many people who love you - be strong and smile!

Josie Pinder

What constitutes domestic abuse?

Domestic abuse is a pattern of aggressive or controlling behaviours carried out within the context of an intimate relationship. These behaviours can involve physical, sexual, financial or emotional abuse and can happen to anybody regardless of sexual preference, race, culture, age, lifestyle or class. It is more commonly instigated by a man towards a woman. Domestic abuse includes both threats and actual instances of physical violence.

Why is he abusive?

An abuser's behaviour stems from his values and beliefs about intimate relationships. He believes that he is entitled to certain privileges that do not apply to his partner. He sees her as a possession rather than an equal and exercises abuse in order to gain power and control over her.

Types of abuse

Financial - taking money from you, making you ask for money, giving you an allowance, stopping you from working or from keeping a job

Emotional - playing mind games, putting you down, calling you names, and making you feel bad about yourself

Sexual - treating you as a sexual object, forcing you to have sex, doing sexual things against your wishes, attacking sexual parts of your body

Physical - hitting, slapping, pushing, punching, biting, twisting arms, using weapons, grabbing, beating, choking

Isolation - controlling what you do, where you go, and who you see and talk to

Using male privilege - treating you like a servant, making all the 'big' decisions

Intimidation - making and carrying out threats, throwing objects, threatening to commit suicide, hurting/injuring animals, threatening to take children

Using children - using children to cause guilt, giving messages to children, turning children against you, using visitation rights to harass you

Spiritual abuse - using God/scripture to control and use you, using spiritual authority to control and manipulate you

Recognising the signs

If you are experiencing any of the following then it's likely you are being abused, says the domestic abuse charity, Refuge:

- Is he jealous and possessive?
- Does he cut you off from family and friends and try to isolate you?
- Does he have sudden mood changes - charming one minute and abusive the next?
- Does he control your life? (e.g. money, who you should see, what you should wear)

- Does he monitor your movements?
- Does he blame you for the abuse?
- Does he humiliate or insult you in front of others?
- Does he verbally abuse you?
- Does he constantly criticise you?
- Does he use anger and intimidation to frighten you and to make you comply with his demands?
- Does he tell you you're useless and couldn't cope without him?
- Has he threatened to hurt you or people close to you if you leave?
- Do you change your behaviour to avoid making him angry?
- Does he force you to have sex when you don't want to?

If you are being abused, call the free-phone National Domestic Violence Helpline on 0808 2000 247 (run in partnership between Refuge and Women's Aid). www.domesticviolence.co.uk

Rape Crisis: 0808 802 9999; www.rapecrisis.org.uk
Women's Aid: www.womensaid.org.uk
Abundant Life Ministries: www.alm.org.uk
http://thisisabuse.direct.gov.uk/

You may feel unsure of whether behaviours displayed by your partner within your relationship are severe enough to be classed as 'abuse' but worry they may worsen. Or perhaps you've started a relationship with someone new; you may be experiencing early warning signs that abuse may follow. If you feel uneasy, suggest taking a step back, to look at things between you more objectively.

Here are some early signs of control:

- Too much too soon. He pushes for closeness and does not allow you to go at a pace that's comfortable for you.
- He changes expectations or guidelines so that you're left feeling confused as to how to please him.
- He puts down and speaks disrespectfully of former partners and/or has a negative attitude towards women.

If any of the above attitudes or behaviours make you feel uncomfortable, let him know as soon as possible that it's unacceptable. If he continues, make it clear that the relationship cannot go forward until the attitude/ behaviour is addressed. If he still continues or resorts to other inappropriate behaviour, this is a sign that he's not ready to 'own' his problem and be committed to a path of change and growth.

Control doesn't equal love and respect. Controlling people are often inherently insecure - when they inflict their wishes on someone else it gives them a sense of control.

Thank you for reading my story. I hope this has shown you that domestic abuse is a far more common issue than it should be, and that if you're a victim, approaching domestic abuse organisations for help will be without judgement. You are strong, and you can regain control of your life with the proper support.

I know this because I was once a victim. Now, I'm a survivor.